Oneida

These things shall be! A loftier race
Than e'er the world has known shall rise
With flame of freedom in their souls
And light of science in their eyes.

New arts shall bloom of loftier mould,
And mightier music thrill the skies,
And every life shall be a song,
When all the earth is paradise.

John Addington Symonds (1840–93)

Oneida
Utopian Community to Modern Corporation

MAREN LOCKWOOD CARDEN

SYRACUSE UNIVERSITY PRESS

Copyright © 1998 by Syracuse University Press
Syracuse, New York 13244-5160

All Rights Reserved

Syracuse University Press Edition 1998

98 99 00 01 02 03 6 5 4 3 2 1

Originally published in 1969 by The Johns Hopkins Press.

The paper used in this publication meets the minimum requirements of American National Standard for Information Sciences—Permanence of Paper for Printed Library Materials, ANSI Z39.48-1984. ∞™

Library of Congress Cataloging-in-Publication Data

Carden, Maren Lockwood.
Oneida : utopian community to modern corporation / Maren Lockwood Carden.—1st Syracuse University Press ed.
p. cm.
Originally published: Baltimore : Johns Hopkins Press, 1969.
Includes bibliographical references and index.
ISBN 0-8156-0523-4 (alk. paper)
1. Oneida Community. 2. Oneida Ltd. I. Title.
HX656.05C3 1998
335'.974764—DC21 98-6533

Manufactured in the United States of America

To
my parents,
Marjory Kimberley Lockwood and James Leonard Lockwood,
who together have
created their own utopia

Contents

List of Illustrations

Acknowledgments

Many persons have helped me to reconstruct Oneida's history and to prepare this book. My investigations into the Oneida Community began at the suggestion of Professor Margaret Cussler, who introduced me to the general field of reform movements and stimulated my interest in Oneida. Later she and Professors Francesca Cancian, Llewellyn Gross, George C. Homans, Edward O. Laumann, Thomas F. Pettigrew, Victoria Steinitz, and Mark van de Vall contributed insightful observations and valuable ideas to the developing study. Further important substantive suggestions for clarifying and sharpening the manuscript were made by Miss Barbara Parmelee, of The Johns Hopkins Press.

The American Philosophical Society, Radcliffe College, the State University of New York at Buffalo, and Boston University contributed welcome funds toward the completion of the research.

People at Oneida have maintained the community's high traditions of hospitality and concern for scholarship in welcoming me and enriching my understanding of the community. Mr. Pierrepont T. Noyes, president of Oneida Ltd., granted permission for the research, discussed the contemporary community with me, and allowed me to quote from a number of published and unpublished sources. Mrs. Florence Ackley Owen, whose great-grandfather was one of the first Perfectionists to settle at Oneida, combined the old Community's virtues of integrity and knowledgeability in giving me information about Oneida. Many others coopererated in the field work, commented on the analysis, allowed me to read and to quote from private manuscript material. These include the honorary chairman of the board, Mr. Miles E. Robertson, the late Mr. Robert Wayland-Smith, Mr. Jerome Wayland-Smith, Mrs. Jane Kinsley Rich, Mrs. Adèle Noyes Davies, the late Mr. Stephen R. Leonard, Mr. Stephen R. Leonard, Jr., the late Miss Margaret E. Kinsley. Mrs. Dorothy Ackley, Mr. and Mrs. Hamilton Allen, Mr. and Mrs. Henry G. Allen, and Mrs. Cherie Hinds Sewall.

I wish to thank Mr. Pierrepont T. Noyes for permission to use the photographs reproduced on the dust jacket of the book and on pages 10, 44, 55, 75, 82, 105, 149, 176, and 187; Mrs. Imogen Noyes Stone for those on pages 5 and 90; and Mr. Stephen R. Leonard, Jr., for the case illustration, which came from the collection of the late Stephen R. Leonard. Mr. Harry S. Jones very kindly took the photographs of Kenwood which enhance the account of the modern community.

Miss Elma S. Leavis, Mrs. Shelby T. Shrigley, and Mrs. Judith W. Augusta typed the manuscript with all the patience and care one would want. Mrs. Judith O. Noyes was on hand at Oneida as a skilled research assistant whenever she was needed.

To all these and to others at Oneida and elsewhere who, by giving information, ideas, and encouragement, have helped to make this a fascinating project, I give warm thanks.

Maren Lockwood Carden

Introduction

In 1988 ownership of the material remains of the nineteenth century religious utopia, Oneida, passed to a recently-formed not-for-profit organization, Oneida Community Mansion House. OCMH received the rambling two hundred room Victorian Gothic Mansion House and surrounding land (valued at about $4 million) from Oneida Ltd., the business founded at the dissolution of the original community. The people who founded OCMH had long and happy associations with Oneida; many traced descent from the original community; and they were deeply committed to preserving Oneida's intellectual as well as its material heritage. The house today represents three historical periods: first, Oneida's thirty-two years as an extraordinarily successful and daring religious commune; second, its many decades as an informal, idealistic community that prospered alongside the modern corporation, the Oneida Community, Limited, founded at the first Community's demise; and third, the contemporary museum. This book describes the nonmaterial remains of the first two periods.

THE ONEIDA COMMUNITY. John Humphrey Noyes founded the Oneida Community in 1848 with about fifty followers all of whom were determined to practice his Perfectionist Christianity. By the time the Community was disbanded in 1881 it had almost three hundred members supported by agriculture, trap manufacture, and other light industries. Settled in western New York State, the birthplace of many religious and reform movements (and a dozen or more communes), the Perfectionists typified the nineteenth-century communal movement in several ways. They represented the belief that, in the new American nation, people could create a perfect society. They wanted to change the larger society by example, not by direct reform: if they created a small-scale ideal society, the nation as a whole would copy their example. And they took advantage of available land and the prevailing economic optimism to urge members to abandon their old lives for financially-risky new ones.

Yet Oneida's continuing fascination does not lie in its contribution to the larger communal movement. Its appeal lies in its exemplification of a reality outside the one in which we live. We see this different reality in its religious orientation. The nineteenth century was a time when people sought religious experiences; they awaited God's spirit; and they discussed Christian belief. Noyes's Perfectionist teachings owed much to his own searchings and his discussions with fellow students and ministers. He announced that sin could be vanquished and that suffering and death must soon disappear. He reinterpreted other orthodox beliefs including those beliefs relating to man's depravity, justification by faith, the second coming, the kingdom of heaven, Satan, and biblical authority.

An examination of the Community which Noyes and his followers founded to practice Perfection raises for us the question of what lies at the center of a fulfilled life? Should our quest be for spiritual growth, for improved personal relationships, or for material comforts? For people at Oneida the answer was spirituality. People joined the Community because they fully believed John Humphrey Noyes's radical interpretation of Christian Perfectionism. These three hundred people strove for perfection as earnestly as any group of monks or nuns—by means of prayer, by religious study, by holding themselves open to

God's spirit. They believed that once they achieved spiritual perfection they could gradually perfect their behavior. People joined Oneida to become spiritually and behaviorally perfect.

One of the most fundamental questions they had to answer in their practical, community-based search for perfection grew out of the question of social order. How were they to balance individual and group interests? First, they made the ideals of self-perfection and commitment to the Community central to community life. Second, they pointed out that self-perfection was not simple individualism: it included active contributions to the group's welfare. Third, they made sure that these principles underlay all Community practices.

Their comprehensive, ambitious goal of creating a brand-new society encouraged, even obliged, members to explore many new, potentially enriching experiences. The practices which the Perfectionists introduced in their thirty-two year effort to translate spiritual perfection into behavior seemed strange and even bizarre to nineteenth-century observers. They often seem so to people today. Yet, despite the dangers of outsider opposition and of internal rebellion (and always with an air of middle-class respectability) the Perfectionists introduced many unusual practices. They required that members seek many sexual partners, introduced "male continence" as a means of birth control, practiced eugenics, reorganized traditional child rearing, ranked all members according to their degree of spirituality, and created a complex system of social control. They adopted new attitudes toward sickness, death, male-female relationships, parent-child relationships, and the allocation of work. The Perfectionists were so convinced that these practices made their's the perfect life that only in the Community's very last year did anyone question its permanence.

John Humphrey Noyes did not create these practices, or the principles upon which they were based, out of whole cloth the year he founded Oneida. Like the founder of any successful organization, he drew upon years of experience and careful planning. When Noyes attended theological school at Andover and, later, at Yale, he had rejected traditional Calvinist teachings on man's sinfulness for the Wesleyan doctrine of holiness. Wesleyan holiness was expounded in moderate terms by preachers like Charles Grandison Finney, the founder of Oberlin College, and in less moderate terms by people like Noyes. The men and women who joined Noyes at Oneida had studied Perfectionists' writings for years. They attended meetings and even occasionally adopted semicommunal living arrangements. Beginning in 1844 Noyes had tried a form of communalism with a few followers in Putney, Vermont. There he learned, among other things, that those who shared marriage partners could be forced out of town. But this and his other experiences enabled him to create a successful community at Oneida beginning in 1848.

An examination of the practices Noyes introduced at Oneida encourages us to reevaluate many social institutions. The family is one of these. Under the system of "complex marriage," members were expected to love everyone in the community equally and to seek out many sexual partners; birth control was required and the men, through "continence" (*coitus reservatus*), provided it. During the community's last ten years, children were deliberately conceived under a eugenics program for which couples were carefully selected. Children were raised communally and mother love was forbidden. The traditional division of labor between men and women was changed to bring about some sharing of domestic and nondomestic responsibilities in the businesses, the printing office, the kitchen, and the children's quarters.

Any detailed examination of how family functions could be fulfilled in these ways raises new questions: Was it as difficult to love many marriage partners as to be faithful to one? How did men react to having intercourse without ejaculation? What was women's experience in the encounters? How much or how little do we know about the varieties of sexual experience? Should mothers, fathers, couples, or a group care for children? Was Oneida's perception of what constituted equality the same as ours? Is such equality possible? Can eugenics work? Is it moral?

When members depart from convention in so many and such dramatic ways they must tailor special, perhaps more rigorous, means for social control. The Perfectionists criticized major and minor lapses in open meetings, letters, and even in Community publications. Those criticized confessed their failures. Their lives were so open to public scrutiny that every personal weakness was seen and collusion to hide weakness virtually impossible. Offenders lost privileges: they might be moved to less rewarding jobs or they might be denied sexual privileges. Recalcitrants left. The Perfectionists' experience encourages us to evaluate these methods of social control. It also makes us think about the sorts of conditions under which social controls are most, and least, needed.

Virtues as well as vices deserve our attention. The greatest virtue lay in spirituality. Members were ranked from least to most spiritual in a hierarchy called the "ascending fellowship." Only in a small, homogeneous, essentially public group could people agree upon such a hard-to-measure quality as spirituality. Spiritually superior people exist in modern complex society but we can scarcely identify them. At Oneida the Perfectionists could give the most respect to those highest in the ascending fellowship. They rewarded such people with jobs like that of editor of the Community periodical. Yet one wonders whether privilege went only to the spiritually superior and why Noyes's relatives tended to rank high.

Curiously, neither higher nor lower ranking members seemed bothered by the practice of sharing property. Criticisms mention almost every subject except an unwillingness to share property—unwillingness to work, exclusive love relationships, lateness, dourness, lack of courtesy, and excessive friendliness toward outsiders. Sometimes people were criticized for not wanting to change rooms in the Mansion House, but no one ever questioned the idea that the room was community property. The horticulturist was admired for his high-quality fruit and the chain-maker for his or her speed, but no one disputed that the resulting products belonged to everyone. Perhaps there is some connection between participants' acceptance of communalism and the community's overall prosperity, for in Oneida's later years, the only people who were not well off were the hundred or so paid, mostly seasonal, workers who were brought to Oneida by the day from neighboring settlements.

Oneida's experience also tells us about the earthly practicalities of what the Perfectionists believed was the divinely inspired leadership of John Humphrey Noyes. He attracted followers by his extensive religious knowledge and by the theological system he formed out of it. He selected members so carefully that very few ever questioned him. His chosen lieutenants compensated for his weak points. His social aloofness allowed members to see in him perhaps nonexistent qualities. And he was sexually attractive.

The people who joined Oneida and stayed adjusted themselves completely to its unconventional practices, but observers have wondered about what personal motives attracted them. Some will say that we do not know enough to assess retrospectively the members' psyches. Others will argue that in any case such judgment is useless because later judges cannot cast aside their historical and social biases about such things as normal religious strivings. But we still wonder, are there any fundamental differences between people who lead conventional lives and those who lead unconventional ones? Or are there differences among people attracted to unusual careers, those who spend their lives in cultures different from their own, and who join unconventional religious groups?

Most social situations and social relationships require complex explanations—and Oneida is no exception. We have no single or easy answers to the questions of why Noyes was an effective leader, why complex marriage worked, why members had no difficulty sharing property, or why the community eventually disbanded. Similarly there are many interrelated factors which explain Oneida's successful transition to a joint-stock company.

THE ONEIDA COMMUNITY, LIMITED. When, in 1881, the Oneida Community disbanded and reorganized itself as a joint-stock company, it was organized into two distinct groups of people: management and workers. Management officials lived and worked in or near the Mansion House in the area later called Kenwood. Workers lived and worked in the area later called Sherrill. Since the division remained important, I shall treat the two groups separately.

Management consisted of former Community members and, later, their descendants. Now paid for their work, they ran the old Community's businesses and they led thoroughly conventional lives married to former Community women. These management officials lived in apartments within the Mansion House or, in later years, in houses they built on adjacent land in Kenwood. For several generations after the breakup these people ran the Oneida Community, Limited as an extended family firm. Significant numbers of outsiders were brought in after the 1920s, but even in the 1960s a number of descendants, including the president, P. T. Noyes, a grandson of John Humphrey Noyes, were still employed in management.

From the last decade of the nineteenth century to the mid-twentieth century, company officials and their wives created a tremendously strong sense of community in Kenwood. Their success owed much to their descent from the old Community, their shared past, their shared involvement in the company, and their shared social life. At the same time, because they lived and worked so closely, and because they planned to continue to live that way, people in Kenwood and the company management treated seriously the question of getting along with each other. The management team drew on the strengths of lifetime friendships and accommodated to interpersonal frictions. Even when retired they remained involved in company affairs. Kenwood residents' experiences prompt us to consider the benefits of living in close communities and encourage us to explore how such a community could be created today.

The descendants' mutual commitment derived in part from shared fears of public ridicule about their parents' practice of complex marriage. They lessened these fears not only by staying together in Kenwood but also by adopting very conventional American family patterns. The most striking feature of these new families is how traditionally they interpreted gender roles. Men worked in the company; women cared for the children and the home. Men's lives revolved around work and work-related recreation; women's lives revolved around catering to men's needs and rearing children. Even in the 1960s Kenwood wives followed traditional roles, although the younger generation of women was thinking about combining a career with marriage. Whether we look at the 1960s or the 1890s, we can examine marriages in which men and women lived in separate spheres.

People in Kenwood sought to define what their community represented. Unlike the *old* Community, theirs had not been founded as a perfect or even a better society; but people knew that their community was different. Pierrepont Burt Noyes, a son of the founder and the greatly admired leader of the company from the 1890s to the 1930s, defined this difference. He described a new idealism involving group harmony, teamwork, mutual concern, personal improvement, and relative equality. His ideals, unlike his father's, were not newly minted: they were extracted from an existing system to guide the Kenwood and management parts of the new Oneida. They were an example of an ideology.

For Oneida's workers P. B. Noyes had a different vision. Concern for workers' welfare would distinguish the company. Under him the Oneida Community, Limited became an example of paternalistic or welfare capitalism. He and his enthusiastic management team worked to provide high wages, generous benefits, and good working conditions. They made sure that in the village-sized but legally constituted city of Sherrill solid, attractive houses were built across the main road from the factory. They provided a clubhouse for indoor recreation, sports fields, a place to swim and boat, and a golf course. They supported local schools and helped build churches. And, as a result, they drew enormous respect and admiration from the workers.

The Oneida Community, Limited found it could provide these benefits to workers while making a profit. Their success and other companies' experiences make us think about business objectives. By what criteria should a company be judged? Should it seek profit, worker satisfaction, or both? How explicit can it make these objectives? A certain amount of worker satisfaction correlates with company profit but how does a company identify the "best" balance between human and financial concerns? And what additional human concerns ought a company to consider today?

Whether they were associated with the plant or with management, people working for the company and their families found the Sherrill and Kenwood communities very pleasant and congenial places to live and work. They still are so today. Well over a hundred years ago, a different Oneida offered a very different way of life. The final question this book raises is whether people in either of Oneida's stages found a way of life superior to most.

Introduction to the Original Edition

A hundred years ago the Oneida Community was a prosperous religious utopia hidden in the rolling farmland of upstate New York. It professed to be a perfect society based on a degree of idealism supposedly unknown in the secular world. Perfect or imperfect, the Oneida Community survived for thirty-two years and has achieved fame as one of the few long-lived utopian communities.

John Humphrey Noyes, who founded Oneida in 1848, taught an extreme form of Christianity known as Perfectionism. His elaborate theology justified the assertion of individual perfection and the belief that it could be expressed in an actual community.

He organized the Oneida Community according to Perfectionist principles which, although he never stated them specifically, involved two central ideals or values: self-perfection and communalism. Self-perfection entailed the improvement of one's spiritual state, one's character, and one's intellect; communalism entailed sharing everything with the Community. In keeping with the ideal of self-perfection, members studied Noyes's theology, they prayed, they heard group criticism and acted upon it, and they participated in educational schemes. In keeping with the communal ideal, they combined all their capital and property and lived together in the large rambling Mansion House. All shared the work on the Community's farm and in its several enterprises, including a highly successful trap-making business. Communalism went even farther: monogamous marriage was abolished and Oneida was transformed into one large "family" practicing "complex marriage." Under this system, monogamous relationships among the more than two hundred adult members were forbidden, and theoretically any couple could engage in sexual intercourse. Oneida's experiment in sexual relations brought the Community much notoriety and evoked many salacious fantasies, but in practice, complex marriage, like other aspects of communalism, imposed many hardships and often severely tested the members' commitment to Perfectionism.

In later years, after Oneida had become a symbol of the successful utopia, its members began to neglect the Community's original ideals. The neglect continued largely unnoticed for more than ten years. Then, in 1879, a serious conflict split the Community into two opposing factions. Unable to resolve their differences, members set about transforming Oneida into a joint-stock company—the Oneida Community, Limited—which they owned and managed. For the non-Perfectionist "outsiders" who were employed in the Community industries and farm, little was changed, but the "breakup" caused a drastic reorganization of the ex-members' lives. Only in their daily work, which involved managing or otherwise contributing to the new company's businesses, did their routines remain relatively unchanged. Many of the ex-members abandoned Perfectionist beliefs, and all gave up complex marriage. Property was divided, and each monogamous family managed its own finances, using money received for work and from stock dividends to pay for board and room in the Mansion House and for other personal necessities. The return to the secular world was virtually complete. Utopia had been abandoned.

During the years immediately following Oneida's reorganization, the new company's economic situation deteriorated. Emigration, inadequate leadership, national economic crises, and demoralization resulting from the apparent failure of the old Community caused many ex-members to fear for their livelihood. However, fifteen years after the breakup, Pierrepont Burt Noyes, a son of the founder, returned to reinvigorate the community industries. Soon he had restored economic stability.

After the breakup, management officials, their families, and older retired ex-members continued to live in the Mansion House, where they occupied private apartments but took meals together in a common dining room. The adjacent land was reserved for their use, and once P. B. Noyes had restored confidence in the company, individual families built private houses there. Work and social life revolved around this distinct geographical area, Kenwood. Children went to local public schools and then to college. Their parents often visited nearby towns and occasionally made an excursion by train to New York, but for the most part, entirely by choice, life centered upon Kenwood. In this isolated community two hundred of the ex-members and their descendants shared their work and their leisure time. They formed a cohesive group well suited to adopt the new idealism introduced by P. B. Noyes. Like his contemporaries, he had no faith in the old religious beliefs and made no effort to revive Perfectionism. Instead, he presented Perfectionist values or ideals in a thoroughly modified form. Personal improvement, unpretentious living, approximate equality, commitment to the community, team work, and corporate harmony represented his conception of their "ideal society."

The majority of male ex-members and descendants living with their families in Kenwood worked in the management of the Oneida Community, Limited. Others were retired, and a few held skilled or unskilled jobs in Oneida's several industries. Gradually "outsiders," or non-descendants, married into the Kenwood community or were brought in to fill management posts, but for many years, Kenwood was peopled by descendants from the original Perfectionists' family.

Outside Kenwood, on the other side of Oneida Creek, factory workers and farm employees lived in the growing settlement that eventually became incorporated as Sherrill. As the businesses associated with Oneida's farm produce were gradually replaced by manufacturing enterprises, Sherrill grew into a small industrial community. Noyes extended his idealistic objectives to the factory workers who lived there, but these aims contrasted with those he sought to realize in Kenwood: they amounted to bettering the lives of workers and their families. In the factories he constantly improved wages, working conditions, and fringe benefits; he also made Sherrill a charming, prosperous community consisting largely of privately owned homes—a far cry from the comfortable but dreary uniformity of many company towns. Noyes's efforts to improve workers' conditions may not have put him ahead of the benevolent industrialists of his day, but he certainly belonged in their vanguard.

Although management concerned itself with the Oneida factories, the Kenwood community remained the heart of Oneida. Bonds of common interest and lineage united its members and helped to create a strong sense of family. It was from this general feeling of identification that Noyes derived the new ideals which, for years, many Kenwood inhabitants tried hard to practice. Gradually, however, as in the old Community, idealism was neglected. This second period of idealism has been declining for over thirty years and today, in effect, is over.

Both the original Community and its successor can be looked upon as special sorts of organizations, possessing the unusual goals of putting their own values or ideals into practice. The first Community made the implementation of Perfectionist ideals its primary objective and relegated other necessary goals like economic success to a secondary position. Such an organization, founded specifically to implement in its social structure a particular set of ideals is what I shall call utopia or a utopian community.[1]

[1] Others have seen ideals or values as central to the concept of utopian community. For example, describing a contemporary community, one of the Israeli kibbutzim, Melford E. Spiro finds the kibbutz member "dedicated to the social, economic, and national ideals for which the kibbutz stands. These ideals were

During its second idealistic period, Oneida did not have a formally constituted social organization. The community was a highly cohesive but informal organization which closely overlapped with the management of the Oneida Community, Limited. When P. B. Noyes introduced idealistic objectives to the Kenwood "society," he in fact selected ideals that the residents had already accepted more or less consciously. His was not, therefore, a utopian community in the sense in which I have defined the term. Instead it was what I shall call an ideological community—one whose ideals were already implemented in the social structure before Noyes defined them.[2]

To retain its idealism, each community had to find ways to maintain members' commitment to the ideals and to the organization in which they were represented. This study analyzes, in the context of the interrelationships between individual and organizational interests, how the utopian

---

formulated before [the community] came into being and, indeed, it was founded with the purpose of bringing these ideals into being." And later, the "social structure [of the kibbutz] was designed to implement its values." *Kibbutz: Venture in Utopia* (Cambridge: Harvard University Press, 1956), pp. 11, 61.

[2] "Ideology" is one of the social science concepts which has acquired several possible meanings or sets of meanings. The word generally applies to the study of ideas within a specific social setting (usually a whole society) and the effect of these ideas upon social development. This interpretation is usually accompanied by some combination of the following implications: that the ideas under study may be distorted, perhaps radically, and that people in the society may or may not be conscious of that distortion; that the ideas may be used to explain complex social phenomena, possibly through oversimplification; and that the ideas are generally seen as helping individuals and groups to make social and political choices.

Here I shall be using the term ideology to mean the specific ideals which leaders or other Kenwood residents thought to be representative of Oneida. Some people distorted the ideals; some believed that all changes in the community were the result of changes in the ideals; and some used the ideals to guide decisions relating to the community. The community whose members have created this ideology is called an ideological community.

Oneida, and later the ideological Oneida, managed to keep alive an unusual set of ideals, or values, among a small group of people over a long period of time. The study also suggests some conditions that contribute to the success and failure of utopias. It does not, however, make more than an occasional comparison of Oneida with other utopias because experimental communities are so varied that a comparison of them would require a whole book in itself.

In collecting information about Oneida and its participants I have used a variety of research techniques. For information about the old Community one must rely exclusively upon written materials. For this reason, it is fortunate that Community members kept, as John Humphrey Noyes urged, a detailed written history of their communal and individual progress. The periodicals, pamphlets, and books that the Community produced are listed in the Bibliography. Most of the old Community's manuscript materials were preserved after the breakup. At the beginning of this century, they were handed over to a historical committee which, over the years, added to the collection personal documents donated by the original members and their descendants. Regrettably, some twenty years ago the present community decided to destroy the greater part of these official records and personal accounts. "Half a room full" of paper was burned. Despite this loss, I have managed to locate a number of surviving manuscripts. These letters, diaries, biographical accounts, statistical compilations, and first-hand descriptions of Community life have supplemented and shed new light on published accounts.

Written material about the Oneida Community, Limited, is also available.[3] There are a number of brief and two lengthy biographical accounts, a company-sponsored history,

[3] Various commercial considerations, described at the beginning of Chapter V, caused the company to change its name to Oneida Ltd. in 1935. Technically, therefore, this part of the research concerned first the Oneida Community, Limited, and then Oneida Ltd.

and a succession of Kenwood periodicals produced intermittently since 1894. Several people have kept statistical data on such matters as births, deaths, marriages, and places of residence. Others have preserved letters, newspaper clippings, a lively annotated summary of the board of directors' minutes, personal accounts, and diaries.

Present descendants know little more about the old Community than that which has already been published, but they can offer a good deal of information about the present Oneida. Since Kenwood is a stable community where many people have lived throughout their working lives and on into retirement, its residents can describe, more or less accurately, the years since 1900. I questioned in detail approximately one-third of the adult residents. Forty-four individuals, carefully selected according to age, sex, marital status, and descendant or outsider status, described in tape-recorded interviews their personal reasons for being at Oneida and their feelings about the community. Others, including the company president, the past president, and the active and retired treasurers, were asked to describe their views of the firm as it related to Kenwood. In addition, management officials who lived outside Kenwood, descendants working in the plant and living in Sherrill, college students, and descendants and outsiders who had been brought up in Kenwood but had left were all asked in formal interviews about Oneida and about their reactions to the idea of living and working there.

Although the research was not sponsored by the company, I had official permission to conduct it. By actually living in the Mansion House and eating in the common dining room I was able to observe and be observed and to talk freely with many Kenwood men and women during my first summer-long visit and succeeding shorter stays. In this middle-class community of people accustomed to scholarly work, the project was, on the whole, well received.

I have been scrupulously careful to keep confidences and to avoid repeating anything that may hurt a particular person. In presenting the results I have preserved respondents' anonymity by not footnoting any of the quotations from interviews, although occasionally the person interviewed is identified in the text.

Any highly theoretical sociological presentation of the conclusions from this extensive field work and library research would subsume beneath its abstract concepts much information about the way Oneida operated. Such an account, furthermore, inevitably would omit those aspects of community life which were not directly related to the formal concepts within which the analysis was made. Rather than present an incomplete but rigorously theoretical account, I have chosen to give a comprehensive view of the workings of the original Community and its successor.

Oneida

I
The Oneida Community: Utopia

John Humphrey Noyes. A few months before John Humphrey Noyes founded the Oneida Community, his mother wrote to one of her daughters, "I am ready to ask sometimes, Do I dream, or is this all a reality? If John thinks to maintain his position and carry out his principles in the face of a world in arms, it will be the greatest miracle the world ever saw."[1] Although she was a convert to Perfectionism and a loyal mother, she could not subdue her incredulity at the momentous social and religious changes her son proposed.

From Noyes's entry into divinity school sixteen years before, his intellectual development had inexorably led him to those convictions which shocked his mother. At that time religious and social ideas were beginning to change into the more liberal philosophies of the present day. But Noyes's views were far ahead of those common in the 1840's. He taught that one should follow only the inspired spirit of the Bible, not the letter of its law. To him, there were no absolute standards of morality. What is right for one time is wrong for another: it is a higher form of ethics to be responsible to oneself than to an external set of rules. In less specifically religious terms, although not without religious justification, he insisted that life is supposed to be happy.

[1] George Wallingford Noyes, ed., *John Humphrey Noyes: The Putney Community* (Oneida, N.Y.: By the author, 1931), p. 315.

Men, and women too, should cultivate and desire the joys of all experience—including the joys of sexual intercourse. With regard to matters ranging from religion to sex, this nineteenth-century prophet rejected the conventions of his day and often anticipated more than a century of change.

John Humphrey Noyes's uneventful childhood promised none of the drama of his later years. He was born in Brattleboro, Vermont, where his father ran a successful store and trading post. John Noyes, Sr., was a college graduate with an active mind that impressed the other townspeople. By the time his son was born in 1811, Noyes, Sr., ranked among Brattleboro's elite. Four years later he was elected from southern Vermont to the House of Representatives. This took him to Washington for two years. Then, although he was only fifty-three years old, he left politics, sold his business in Brattleboro, and retired. A few years later he settled with his wife and eight children in Putney, a small town ten miles to the north of Brattleboro.

From the age of nine, young John was enrolled in nearby private schools and, as was common in those times, was ready for college at the age of fifteen. Dartmouth was chosen. In 1830 he graduated with high honors and searched for an appropriate occupation. At first he entered the law office of his brother-in-law, Larkin G. Mead. Although not unsuccessful at the law, he decided after a year to become a minister. His conversion occurred unexpectedly at a protracted revival meeting in Putney, but he had had plenty of earlier encouragement to take this path. His mother was devoutly religious. She taught her children to read daily from the New Testament and urged them, after the fashion of the day, to seek a conversion experience. She had always hoped that John would be called to the ministry.

Noyes spent a year at the Andover Theological Seminary reading and studying, all the zeal of his conversion still within him. The atmosphere proved too conservative, however, and he considered transferring to the more liberal divinity school at Yale. Uncertain what to do, he opened his Bible at random—a common custom of that time for one seeking guidance—and came upon the words, "Fear not ye: for I know that ye seek Jesus, which was crucified. He is not here." [2] Noyes was convinced. In the fall of 1832 he set off for Yale to seek the true Jesus.

While studying at the Yale seminary, Noyes joined a local New Haven church, one of the "free churches" that were being founded all over the Northeast by people who disapproved of the practices and teachings of such established denominations as the Presbyterians and the Congregationalists. Most ministers disapproved of the free churches' emotional revival services and their apparently willful interpretations of doctrine. But the same men admitted that their own denominations' revival meetings gave the free churches the example for their highly charged conversion techniques and created the unconventional atmosphere that encouraged people to question established doctrine. The dozen or so members of the group that Noyes joined divided their time between revival meetings and theological discussion. This was fertile soil, in which the seeds of Noyes's radical ideas could grow. Nonetheless, he continued with his studies at Yale and a year after his arrival in New Haven was licensed to preach. His heterodox statements had already caused comment among the students and the faculty, but perhaps the seminary approved his licensing because it expected the next year's study and candidate preaching to distract him from his youthful excesses.

Inside and outside the seminary orthodox ministers were re-evaluating religious beliefs. For example, Nathaniel W. Taylor, one of the liberal faculty members at New Haven, questioned the Calvinist doctrine of man's depravity and complete inability to do good except through God's intervention. God, he said, makes man able to choose be-

[2] Matt. 28:5–6, quoted in John Humphrey Noyes, *Confessions of John H. Noyes, Part I: Confession of Religious Experience: Including a History of Modern Perfectionism* (Oneida Reserve, N.Y.: Leonard & Co., Printers, 1849), p. 6. Part II was never published. In succeeding chapters I shall footnote this as a complete work. Capitals omitted.

tween right and wrong. Some preachers outside the seminary were bolder. They took up the Wesleyan doctrine of holiness, which told man that he could attain a state of perfect love between himself and God. The new idea appealed to many laymen who were accustomed to hearing far more about sin and guilt than about holiness. Consequently, revivalists like James Latourette and John B. Foot, who preached the new doctrine, became popular. Their theology earned them the label of "Perfectionists."

The doctrine of holiness attracted Noyes; the more he studied, the more he was convinced that it should be taken further. Soon after receiving his license to preach he declared that man can be perfect—and that he himself *was* perfect. This assertion led him into violent controversy with his fellow seminarians, who rejected his statement almost unanimously and even suggested that he was insane. As a result of the general opposition to his views and under pressure from the Yale faculty, Noyes gave up his license to preach. The members of the New Haven free church gave him little more support than had the seminary: a majority voted to request that he leave their fellowship.

A twenty-three-year-old discharged from the ministry, Noyes was on his own, almost without followers. His prospects were not encouraging; however, he declared that he would go on to clear Perfectionism's reputation of the "mysticisms and barbarisms" that discredited it and made the new doctrines unacceptable to the world at large.[3] In fact, he was setting out to try to impose his own extremist views upon the whole loosely knit Perfectionist movement. Scarcely had Noyes begun this self-imposed ministry when he attended an annual meeting of ministers and theologians in New York. Among representatives from all over the country he hoped to meet Charles Grandison Finney, the great revivalist who was already preaching his own version of Perfectionism. Eventually, as leader of the movement's more conservative wing, Finney was to found what became known

[3] J. H. Noyes, *Confessions*, pp. 30–31.

In appearance, John Humphrey Noyes
was as conventional as his ideas
were unconventional.

George Wallingford Noyes, ed., The Religious Experience of John Humphrey Noyes *(Macmillan Co.)*

as Oberlin theology. Noyes's efforts to secure an interview with the revivalist failed. Nor was he able to engage other revivalists and ministers in the fervent discussions he hoped would strengthen the influence of Perfectionism—and perhaps his own convictions. No one seemed especially concerned with the matters that to him were of burning interest. Overcome with disappointment, tormented by religious questions, and alone, he sank into despair. For three weeks he wandered about the city, scarcely sleeping or eating. He drank in deliberate rebellion against the abstemious rules of the church. His mind preternaturally active, he struggled with the complexities and implications of Perfectionist thought. He preached Perfectionism to the poor and outcast of the city. His behavior was obviously strange and tormented, but afterward he always asserted that it was neither offensive nor immoral. Finally an acquaintance discovered his plight and reported it to his brother Horatio, who quickly arranged for his return to New Haven. Within a short time Noyes was quite recovered. The incident caused a certain coolness among some of the New Haven Perfectionists, but others remained loyal, and soon most of them had forgotten the incident.

Despite his failure to make any impression on the theologians at the New York meeting, Noyes was determined to seek converts to his version of Perfectionism. He spent the next two years proselytizing in New York State and New England, vigorously arguing about doctrinal differences with competing Perfectionist leaders. For all their rebellion from orthodoxy, none could equal Noyes's catalogue of heresies: the Second Coming had already occurred; man could be perfect; once having attained salvation man could not fall from grace; man should not allow his inner convictions to be overruled by church authority. These ideas were set down in a periodical that Noyes published with James Boyle and Chauncy Dutton. Some six hundred subscribers came to know his views from reading the *Perfectionist*. The paper was published for two years, but within six months Noyes stopped contributing articles because the two other men did not agree with his ideas. After his missionary work in New York and New England, Noyes returned home to his parents in Putney in the the winter of 1836.

The season passed uneventfully as far as the Perfectionist movement at large was concerned. At home, however, Noyes was establishing what was to be the core of his future following. Previously, the members of his own family had rejected his message. They had found his teachings so singular that, like the seminarians, they wondered if he was deranged. They begged him to cease being a homeless wanderer and take up some trade, become a clerk in a counting house, or take a job as a teacher. More recently some of his brothers and sisters had shown greater sympathy for the cause, and this time when he arrived at Putney Noyes devoted all his powers to converting them, confident that with his extensive preaching experience he would eventually succeed. Three of the four Noyes children then at home were converted at this time and remained faithful Perfectionists all their lives. Noyes's mother, too, was convinced, though not without misgivings and periodic backsliding. John Noyes, Sr., disapproved of his son's unsettled ways and rejected his religion. The most that the Putney converts could say of him was that he took an intellectual interest in the Perfectionist theology taught in the so-called Putney Bible School.

In the spring Noyes departed again, eager to advance the cause. This excursion met with more success than his attempt the year before to impress the theologians in New York. Traveling throughout the Northeast, he spoke before many groups and talked to a number of important men. His discussions with the revivalists Charles Grandison Finney and William Green and with the reformers Gerrit Smith and William Lloyd Garrison convinced him for a time that Perfectionist beliefs were being accepted by influential members of the public. A new attack and a new periodical seemed in order. In Ithaca, New York, he began publishing the *Witness,* presenting in its articles his synthesis of Perfectionist ideas—a remarkable achievement for a young man of twenty-six.

The people who accepted Noyes's and other Perfectionist leaders' assertions that it was possible to be perfect generally also believed, in opposition to Noyes, that, once they were convinced of their inner perfection, their outward behavior would automatically be above reproach. This conviction provided some of them with a rationale for holding hands and kissing during their emotional religious meetings. Despite others' disapproval, they put themselves in the way of sexual temptations and were sometimes accused of sexual promiscuity.

Noyes was anxious to keep his own reputation unblemished and to set the highest standards of conventional morality for his own and others' behavior. Yet he had to admit that his own thought was developing along far from conventional lines. His views had been influenced by his passionate attachment to Abigail Merwin, who had been one of his first converts to Perfectionism but who had later rejected his gospel as she refused his attentions. Even when she married in 1837, Noyes could not admit that Abigail was lost to him forever. He came to look upon monogamous marriage as a tyrannical institution that did not exist in heaven and eventually would be abolished on earth. These convictions were expressed in a letter to a disciple, David Harrison. The letter was kept private for some months, but eventually Harrison was persuaded to allow the Perfectionist T. R. Gates to publish it in his magazine, *Battle-Axe and Weapons of War*. It contained these comments:

I will write all that is in my heart on one delicate subject, and you may judge for yourself whether it is expedient to show this letter to others. When the will of God is done on earth as it is in heaven there will be no marriage. Exclusiveness, jealousy, quarreling have no place at the marriage supper of the Lamb. God has placed a wall of partition between man and woman during the apostasy for good reasons; this partition will be broken down in the resurrection for equally good reasons. But woe to him who abolishes the law of the apostasy before he stands in the holiness of the resurrection! I call a certain woman my wife.

She is yours, she is Christ's, and in him she is the bride of all saints.[4]

Publication of the letter caused a sensation among Perfectionists. No one else in the movement had publicly stated that he believed in the exchange of marriage partners. Before this, Noyes's wing of the movement had been limited to those who accepted his extreme statement of the doctrine of holiness. Once his views on marriage became known, many of these followers fell away, and only a small group remained loyal.

Among those who felt the power of Noyes's singular appeal was Harriet A. Holton. She had declared her salvation from sin in 1834 after reading Noyes's article "The Second Coming of Christ." Neither her family nor a minister brought in by her family could reconvert her. Instead she continued to study Noyes's writings and, as she grew more involved, to contribute money to the cause. Her parents were dead, and her grandparents were affluent and generous. Periodically she was able to send Noyes sums of money ranging from twenty to as much as eighty dollars. In 1838, although he had seen relatively little of her, Noyes proposed marriage, and she deemed it appropriate to accept. Noyes's letter of proposal restates his convictions about marriage: he would want his wife to love all men and women; and he asked that neither of them should "monopolize" or "enslave" the other's heart. Marriage, he said; would free him from "many evil surmisings . . . occasioned by [his] celibacy."[5] It would enable them both to pursue God's work more faithfully. He loved her "many desirable qualities" and felt that marriage would make them both happier.[6] Harriet's grandfather failed to make the objections both she and Noyes feared, and in June, 1838, they were married.

[4] Quoted in G. W. Noyes, *J. H. N.: Putney Community,* p. 3. Noyes was not referring literally to his wife, for he did not marry until a year later.

[5] *Ibid.,* pp. 17, 18.

[6] *Ibid.,* p. 18.

A loyal Perfectionist until her death, Noyes's wife Harriet was, in her later years, often referred to as the "Mother" of the Community.

George Wallingford Noyes, ed., John Humphrey Noyes: The Putney Community *(By the author)*

At that time Noyes still thought of the abolition of monogamous marriage as a heavenly condition rather than a hope for heaven on earth. For the moment he was preoccupied with spreading Perfectionist belief and establishing himself more securely as a leader in the movement. Convinced now that he could spread more influence in print than in person, he bought a second-hand printing press. Within a month of his marriage, he, his wife, two of his sisters, and his youngest brother were at work reprinting his earlier articles in a single volume, *The Way of Holiness.* Later they resumed publication of the *Witness,* which had failed for lack of funds more than a year before. Noyes's followers now had three sources in which to read his religious teachings: *The Way of Holiness,* articles in the *Witness,* and articles in the early issues of Boyle's *Perfectionist.*

A NEW PERFECTIONIST THEOLOGY. In 1847 many of Noyes's earliest writings were compiled in a single volume, *The Berean.* Its seventy-four articles, on topics ranging from the "Origin of Evil" through "The Millennium" to "Love of Life," became the Perfectionist bible.[7] Noyes never considered it his last word on religion, however, since he saw perfection as a progressive matter: what was perfect for one period of time was not perfect for another. Numerous supplementary articles appeared in later publications, as did copies of his stenographically recorded informal talks.

In his earlier years especially, Noyes based much of his argument upon biblical exegesis. Like a good seminarian, he marshaled evidence to support his case. Paul was cited most frequently, but references from all the books in the Old and New Testaments were liberally sprinkled throughout his work. By his curiously modern view of the Bible truth is not to be found in its literal statements but in its

[7] The quotation on the title page of *The Berean* explains its name: "[The Bereans] received the word [of the apsotles] with all readiness of mind, and searched the scriptures daily, whether those things were so" (Acts 17:11).

essential spirit: "There is an inexpungable propensity to stick in the letter and come short of the spirit. What better way, then, would there be than [for God] to give men a Bible full of real inspiration, but very imperfect in externals?" [8] The Bible is not "in itself a revelation to men," [9] but needs the interpretation of inspired men to reveal the truth. Noyes saw this as his function. By the exercise of his own intelligence, with God's inspiration, he sought to discover the Bible's meaning for his generation.

In an era in which sects like the Millerites were asserting the imminence of the Second Coming, Noyes asserted that the promised event had occurred almost eighteen hundred years before, at the time of the destruction of Jerusalem. Orthodox belief stated that the Second Coming would inaugurate a period of earthly glory. Noyes agreed. Since those early days all had been in readiness for the eventual perfection of this earthly life. However, after the first generation of Christians (or the primitive church) had died, their successors had strayed from the true path. The nineteenth-century church was "a successor, not of the true primitive church, but of that apostate moiety which forsook the promise of the second coming." [10] Since A.D. 70, therefore, earthly perfection had been possible but had never been achieved.

Noyes claimed, moreover, that even before the Second Coming a few of the early Christians, Paul in particular, had attained earthly perfection. Noyes's opponents responded that this could not be true, that Paul had admitted his own sinfulness in Romans 7. Noyes anticipated this objection and adopted an interpretation first presented to him by Moses Stuart at Andover: he claimed that Paul was not

[8] Alfred Barron and George Noyes Miller, eds., *Home-Talks by John Humphrey Noyes,* I (Oneida, N.Y.: Oneida Community, 1875), 133. Only Volume I was published. In succeeding chapters I shall footnote this as a complete work.

[9] John H[umphrey] Noyes, *The Berean: A Manual for the Help of Those who Seek the Faith of the Primitive Church* (Putney, Vt.: Office of the *Spiritual Magazine,* 1847), p. 37. Italics omitted.

[10] *Ibid.,* p. 297. Italics omitted.

confessing his present sin but his sin before his conversion to Christianity.

Following this interpretation, Noyes argued for the perfection of members of the early Christian church and for the possibility of achieving perfection at the present time. He proposed how this could be done. The spiritual apprehension of Christ's presence in one's soul—that is, a second birth—was not attained easily. It required all the earnest prayer, study of the Bible, and patient waiting on God that were then commonly viewed as the means of attaining a genuine religious experience.

Noyes taught that such a "confession of Christ" gave a spiritual sense of perfection but in no way guaranteed sinless behavior: it referred simply to the quality of one's faith, not to one's deeds. Such a declaration smacked of antinomianism—the heresy that faith alone, exclusive of obedience to the moral law, was sufficient to attain salvation. In reply to this accusation Noyes asserted that one who is "perfectly holy" is not necessarily released

> from all infirmity. . . . We mean by perfect holiness . . . simply that *purity of heart* which gives *a good conscience.* This primary state is attainable by mere faith in the resurrection of Christ. It is in fact the communication of the purity and good conscience of Christ. It may therefore be received instantaneously, and may exist in us antecedently to all external improvement or good works.[11]

"In confessing Christ we receive him as the germ of all righteousness; but this must be expanded in our experience before we can fully realize its benefit." [12] Noyes went on to explain that man has a dual character—an inner and an outer self. When a person has accepted Christ in his soul and thereby become inwardly "perfect," Christ's presence helps the inner self to gain power over the outer self. "We are bound to wait on it [the inner self]—to give it the benefit of our power and wisdom in providing for it good influ-

[11] *Ibid.,* p. 170.

[12] Barron and Miller, *Home-Talks,* p. 154.

ences." [13] Thus a person's actual behavior can be brought more nearly into line with his state of inner perfection. Noyes still believed in free will, however. Christ alone does not save man. Instead He shows him how to save himself. Man's will is "not superseded, but quickened and actuated by Christ's will." [14]

Noyes did not believe that a benevolent God could create evil. Satan, he said, is not God's creature but has existed from eternity. God, for His own purposes, admitted this evil into His creation and at first had made it impossible for man to attain salvation without suffering. However, because of the Second Coming, it is no longer *necessary* to suffer to attain salvation.

> It is the object of God to have as soon as possible, that part of our life that has affinity with the truth, become voluntary under the permanent attraction of the truth; so that there will be no need of suffering.
>
> . . . The truth is, the way of salvation is a pleasurable process. Pleasure is more valuable than pain in its results; and the way that Christ proposes to save us, on the whole, is not by suffering, but by making us happy. The happiest man is the best man, and does the most good.[15]

Noyes believed that any man could choose to become perfect. He also subscribed to the popular belief in the inevitability of social progress. Writing of his ideas when he was still a first-year theological student, he recalled: "I had a glimmering at Andover, that the development of Christianity was *progressive*—and that the destruction of Jerusalem, instead of the birth, ministry or death of Christ, or the day of Pentecost, was the termination of Judaism, and the commencement of mature Christianity." [16] By 1833, his second year in New Haven, he had become convinced that "growth is a principle of God's dispensations—that human nature under divine culture, was gradually ascending

[13] *Ibid.*, pp. 117–18.
[14] *Berean*, p. 173.
[15] Barron and Miller, *Home-Talks*, p. 263.
[16] *Confessions*, p. 8.

heavenward, not only before, but much more after the incarnation of Christ." [17]

Eventually, even death would disappear, Noyes said—although he never stated clearly how this was to come about. "It is certain from the predictions of scripture, that the time is coming when death will be abolished both as to form and substance in this world." [18] When God ultimately reveals His truth, "immortality is to be accessible without death," [19] and man's body as well as his spirit will ascend to heaven as Christ Himself did. In this respect and in many others, Noyes's theology represented an extreme distillation of the nineteenth century's optimism. He believed that mankind would approach nearer and nearer to perfection and true happiness and that eventually the kingdom of heaven would exist on earth.

Noyes also had ideas about the ideal man. He should be spiritual. In seeking inspiration he should go beyond his "own reasonings and . . . the Bible, to invisible spirits." [20] These heavenly members of the primitive church and God Himself would teach him more than he could ever learn from other men.

More than meditation was required of Noyes's ideal man, however. America's activism penetrated Noyes's religious philosophy as deeply as did the era's faith in progress. The ideal man should, like Paul, "keep his face toward God and yet be full of outward activity." [21] Under no circumstances should he be unthinking in this activity, however: man, Noyes believed, has free will which it is his duty to exercise. God will help him, and the Bible will provide inspiration; but ultimately man is responsible for himself through the exercise of his will.

Active and responsible men could be rigid stern puritans, but this was not Noyes's conception of the ideal.

[17] *Ibid.,* p. 9. Italics omitted.
[18] *Ibid.,* p. 36.
[19] J. H. Noyes, *Berean,* p. 483.
[20] Barron and Miller, *Home-Talks,* p. 291.
[21] *Ibid.,* p. 218.

Rather, man should embrace the world. He should continually seek new experiences, and he should accept joyfully all that life has to offer.

At first, Noyes's theology, comprehensive as it was, did not include the notion of the perfect community. He expected Perfectionism to spread through the regular churches and, eventually, to precipitate serious revisions of orthodox doctrine. However, he gradually realized that those churches would never agree with his conception of the perfect marriage and that the form of marriage he advocated was impractical except in an isolated community.

The New Testament statement that "in the resurrection they neither marry, nor are given in marriage" [22] was usually understood to mean that the resurrected man was a sexless creature. Noyes took the opposite view, that sexual relations exist in heaven as on earth. He said the quotation actually referred to the rules, not the fact, of matrimony; it meant that *monogamous* marriage would not exist in the afterlife. Christ had prayed that all His believers would be as one[23]—as one family, said Noyes. Monogamy makes a man or woman unfit to practice the two central principles of Christianity, loving God and loving one's neighbor. "Exclusive attachment" to a spouse turns the attention from God and one's fellow man. It is preferable for a man to love everyone equally and to give his greatest love to God. If there are sexual relations in the kingdom of heaven, then the ideal state is one in which all men are viewed as married to all women. If the kingdom is to be established on earth, it must include such a system of "complex marriage."

Paul's opposition to marriage did not deter Noyes or detract from his admiration of the apostle. Paul's "objections to matrimony," Noyes said, "were not objections to sexual intercourse, but to the distractions and 'troubles of the flesh' incident to a worldly and transitory connection." [24] "He [Paul] looked forward to the resurrection as his home,

[22] Matt. 22:30.
[23] John 17:21–23.
[24] *Berean,* p. 433.

and considering that 'the time was short' that must elapse before his arrival there, he declined encumbering himself with relations that belong only to this world." [25]

While Paul had had to wait until life after death to participate in the ideal marriage system, Noyes felt that mankind had now progressed so far that it could institute ideal marriage on earth. For the time being, however, such an earthly kingdom could be achieved only in a separate society isolated from the secular world. Noyes also believed that the need for a community was justified in other ways. He realized that "the external character of the mass of mankind is, and must be, to a great extent, molded by the society in which they live." [26] Under the pernicious influence of an imperfect society, man could not benefit fully from God's spirit. Thus it was imperative that those "who have obtained eternal life, the root of heart-righteousness, separate themselves more or less from the world, and form a Community for the purpose of establishing good society as the nurse of external character. This is a church: and this completes the machinery for the formation of good men." [27] Here was utopia—where earthly perfection would reach its highest form and Perfectionist ideals would be put into practice.

THE PUTNEY COMMUNITY. When he settled at Putney after his marriage, Noyes did not consider the small group of believers who surrounded him a community. A communal form of society emerged gradually during the following nine years. In this period Noyes occupied himself with publishing and with frequent proselytizing forays. He attended meetings held by other Perfectionists with whom he was competing for leadership of the movement, and he went to the tiny conventions that regional groups organized to promote the cause. Even though his ideas were too extreme to win over large numbers of adherents, he steadfastly continued to

[25] *Ibid.*, p. 432.
[26] Barron and Miller, *Home-Talks*, p. 83.
[27] *Ibid.*

preach the same gospel. Gradually small pockets of Perfectionists in northern New Jersey, northern Vermont, central New York, and central Massachusetts began to look to him as their leader.

These disciples were plied with literature from Putney. The *Witness* was succeeded by the *Perfectionist*,[28] and that in turn by the *Spiritual Magazine*. These periodicals contained many long articles on Noyes's theology. They also recorded the progress of Perfectionist groups throughout the Northeast, encouraged Perfectionists to hold conventions, and gave accounts of any such meetings that took place. Sometimes topics such as social reform, the abolition of slavery, or political questions would head their columns. Sometimes Noyes would comment on the various communal associations of the day, like the Fourier groups or the Skaneateles Community.

Although by 1841 more people were attending to Noyes's ideas, they often interpreted them in ways that clashed with his convictions. If discipline was to be achieved, some form of organization was necessary. The Putney Bible School had been constituted in name only; in 1841 Noyes's Society for Inquiry was formally, although not legally, incorporated. It was still very small. Probably no more than a dozen persons signed the document that undertook to develop and promote the common Perfectionist faith, but it served to train a nucleus of "orthodox" adherents to Noyes's teachings.

Soon the Society took an important step toward community by establishing itself as an economic entity. Early in 1841, eight months before his death, Noyes's father divided his estate among his eight children. A total of almost $20,000 went to the four who belonged to the Putney group; for the first time, Noyes had substantial capital to draw upon. He had operated previously with help from his family and donations from the Perfectionists at large. (His wife had continued to contribute funds and eventually donated over

[28] In 1844, the name was changed to the *Perfectionist and Theocratic Watchman*.

$16,000 to the cause.) Followers who lacked capital could at last be invited to join them. In 1844 the communal aspect of the group was made more formal. Noyes, his brother, and his two brothers-in-law formed a partnership to manage their financial affairs jointly. A year later they remodeled their organization to provide official membership for those who could invest time but not money. With that, the foundation for community was laid: twenty-eight adults and nine children, about half from Putney and half from farther away, belonged to the so-called corporation.

The group supported itself rather precariously by operating two Noyes farms that had been inherited and by running a store. In these enterprises they managed to hold their own, but the $700 or $800 annual loss incurred by the *Perfectionist and Theocratic Watchman* was a worrisome drain on their capital.

All but a few participants lived in one or another of the three houses owned by the Noyes brothers and sisters. They shared their living quarters and their work: the women worked in the household and the men on the farm and in the store. A school was provided for the children. Noyes insisted that men and women should devote three hours a day to reading the Bible, studying theology, and discussing religion. This greatly reduced working hours and further threatened the economy, but Noyes was adamant—religion came first.

Acknowledging that the Community was not to be a democracy, its members voted unanimously for the "theocratic" government of John Noyes. He allowed no opposition to his doctrines or to his organization of the three households. Even his sisters submitted to his choice of husbands for them. One couple in the group was less obedient. Having fallen in love, the two went off privately to be married and were expelled from the Community by Noyes—not because they chose each other but because they had acted without his approval. He commented freely on the characters of all the Community members, criticizing, for example, their pride or worldliness. Not even his mother escaped: he demanded that she humble herself to his will and cease trying to "manage" the family.

As might have been expected, some members felt that this treatment was highhanded. Nine adults and five children left the corporation in 1843 and 1844. They found Noyes's plain speaking too hard to accept and, usually voluntarily, occasionally by request, returned to their former lives. By these means Noyes sifted out a group of tried and utterly faithful disciples. Nineteen adults were in the corporation in 1845. Sixteen of them remained at Putney and then at Oneida until their deaths or until the dissolution of the Oneida Community at the end of 1880.

The American enthusiasm for founding communal associations reached one peak in the mid-1820's and a second between 1842 and 1845.[29] The Putney group flourished in the second of these periods. During that time Noyes's thoughts turned more and more toward the idea of founding a true community. He saw that only complete separation from the world would preserve his followers from contradictory doctrines and allow him to institute the principles of Perfectionism. In addition, in a community the Perfectionists could practice the new form of marriage relationship which he envisioned.

The world at large could easily learn about Noyes's religious principles, but it heard less about his social ideals. The furor that had accompanied the publication of the *Battle-Axe* letter in 1837 had died down, but the public revelation of his views on marriage had only confirmed Noyes's ideas. "From the time of the publication" he felt called "to carry out the doctrine of communism in love." [30]

Until the breakup of the Putney Community in 1847, only those closest to Noyes knew that his concept of a perfect

[29] These communal associations drew their inspiration from utopian socialists like Fourier, Owen, and Cabet, who envisioned the creation of more or less self-contained ideal communities within the larger society. Most of them had disappeared before Marx published his version of communism in the second half of the nineteenth century.

[30] G. W. Noyes, *J. H. N.: Putney Community,* p. 10.

society included the practice of complex marriage. But in the mid-1840's these few waited expectantly for him to declare them ready to overstep the bounds of matrimony and have sexual relations with the husbands and wives of other members. Several men and women were tempted to be unfaithful to their spouses; at least one man and woman are known to have been so. However, when these cases were brought to Noyes's attention, he strictly forbade any sexual intimacy outside marriage, on the grounds that the sense of sin felt by those concerned showed that they were still unconvinced that such a step was God's will.

Noyes himself had to start the new marriage system. In May, 1846, he found himself attracted to a member of the Community, Mary E. Cragin; she returned his feelings. At the same time, Mrs. Cragin's husband George and Noyes's wife admitted their growing affection for each other. After a careful discussion the four agreed they shared the conviction that it was God's will for them to exchange sexual partners—and they did so. Two more couples soon joined them in the practice of complex marriage. Toward the end of 1846, Noyes and his wife, George Cragin and his wife, Noyes's sisters Charlotte and Harriet, and their husbands, John R. Miller and John L. Skinner, stated the principles of their "social union." They agreed to an absolute community of property, including people as well as material possessions. Further, they recognized the ultimate authority of God in all things, and they submitted to the will of John Humphrey Noyes as "the father and overseer whom the Holy Ghost has set over the family thus constituted." [31]

Naturally, these Perfectionists met frequently with the other Putney believers. The whole group gathered each evening at Noyes's home. On Sunday they all listened to Noyes preach in the small chapel they had built themselves, after which they took dinner together. At their work, too, they were in frequent contact with each other. Eventually all the Putney Perfectionists learned that the central members

[31] *Ibid.*, p. 206. Although Noyes and his sisters participated in the system, they of course avoided incestuous relationships.

of their group were exchanging marriage partners. On his missionary trips elsewhere in the country, Noyes himself revealed the new development to a few of his most loyal followers, although he was careful to insist that the practice should not be begun without his approval.

One or two Putney Perfectionists commented on the central members' sexual practices to their friends among the local townspeople. Rumors spread rapidly through Putney. When Noyes was asked what was going on, he described the situation and defended himself vigorously. But the enraged townspeople brought charges of adultery against him, and in November, 1847, Noyes fled to New York City.

For a few months those left behind pursued their joint enterprises. Their lawyer, Noyes's brother-in-law, Larkin G. Mead, advised them on how to proceed. Although he was not a Perfectionist, he was anxious to help the family, and his wife was sympathetic to the cause. The Perfectionists met several times with the townspeople in an effort to restore harmony, but it was evident that for a community such as Noyes envisioned, Putney was not a congenial environment.

THE ONEIDA COMMUNITY. At the time of the attack on the Putney Community, another small group of Perfectionists loyal to Noyes started a communal settlement in Madison County, New York. They had resolved to found an association during the previous September when they were attending a meeting of New York State Perfectionists. Two months later, about a dozen adults and their children were ensconced at the site of an old sawmill on Oneida Creek. The members, including Jonathan Burt, who owned the property, reported their venture to Noyes and invited him to consider transferring the Putney Perfectionists to Oneida. Noyes visited the nascent community and immediately decided to accept the proposal. Having presented the grateful Burt with $500 in cash, he immediately sent for a few members of the Putney group. In the course of the next eighteen months, as accommodations became available, the thirty-one adults and fourteen children who had lived at Putney moved to

Oneida. A few loyal adherents from northern Vermont also moved in. Together the Perfectionists incorporated themselves as the Oneida Association.

During the nineteenth century so many "enthusiasms" swept like fires across the western half of New York State that the region has been called the "burned-over district." The latest representatives in a long line of American communities were established in the area's gently rolling countryside and wooded valleys. Near Groveland a small group of Shakers labored through their daily routines. Throughout the region American enthusiasm for utopian socialism underwent painful empirical tests in the 1820's and the 1840's, when, first, three Owenite communities and, later, seven Fourier phalanxes floundered through brief existences. At Palmyra, Joseph Smith proclaimed that he had received the Mormon revelations from the angel Moroni. A few years later the Millerites, followers of William Miller, anxiously awaited the millennium of 1844. Smith's and Miller's followers eventually created churches of national importance —the Latter-day Saints and the Seventh-day Adventists. Most of the other movements died out within a few years, but that founded by the Perfectionists of Oneida Creek was to last for more than thirty years.

At Oneida John Humphrey Noyes demonstrated how to apply Perfectionist theology to social life. He did not start with blueprints for the size of houses or rules for the rotation of work. To have done so would have been inconsistent with his objection to set procedures. Instead, he ruled according to general principles. Perfectionist doctrine had provided a rationale for establishing the kingdom of heaven on earth. It also provided the two principles that would dominate Community life: individual perfection and communal good.

According to Noyes, anyone who professed inner perfection must work to bring his outer behavior into line with that inner state by improving his moral and spiritual character, by developing his intellectual capacities, and by working to realize all his potentialities. Noyes said that Perfectionism was a school for perfecting character. The Perfectionist must dispel "negative spirits" and must strive instead for a "spirit of love," a "spirit of childlike freedom," and a "spirit that seeks to know and do the will of God." Like spiritual concerns, intellectual endeavor should take precedence over material needs. At Putney, work had not been allowed to reduce the time devoted to study. At Oneida, Noyes urged the toiling utopians to participate in classes even while they were desperately building an economic base during the first lean years. The *Second Annual Report* of 1850 stated their objectives:

> The class of youth, as indeed the whole adult portion of the Community, are encouraged to form themselves into groups and circles for intellectual improvement. In this way the sciences, general literature, music, and the arts, have been to some extent cultivated. We have been closely kept thus far, to our central object, spiritual improvement; but we have no doubt, that as fast as symmetrical development demands, our Association will offer the most perfect advantages for a university education.[32]

The Report went on to state that the Community's idea of education was very broad: "An education for such a destiny [as that of eternal life] must be something more far-reaching, extensive, and practical, than the mere book-knowledge that passes for such in the world." [33] Finally, it reiterated the ideal of self-realization: "We should define it [education] to be, the art or ability of *doing things*; the full development and unimpeded action of all our powers and faculties, both of body and mind: and a complete education thus defined, implies the ability of doing every thing within the range of human capacity." [34]

The second principle or ideal, that of the communal good, was inseparable from the first. Individual perfection

[32] [Oneida] Association, *Second Annual Report of the Oneida Association: Exhibiting Its Progress to February 20, 1850* (Oneida Reserve, N.Y.: Leonard & Co., Printers, 1850), p. 15.
[33] *Ibid.*, p. 16.
[34] *Ibid.*

could be fully achieved only in the context of a community to which each person subjugated all of his selfish interests. Possessiveness with respect to property, time, and other people was forbidden. A member had constantly to strive for self-perfection and to seek "the public spirit" or the "community spirit," fighting "selfishness and egoism" with a "perfectly obedient spirit" through which he "commended himself entirely to Christ and the Church." With enough of the "we" spirit playing about the Community, an "odor of crushed selfishness" would permeate the air in every corner of their common home.

The Oneida Family Register lists names and some personal data for each of the first one hundred and eleven adults who joined the Oneida Association. Many of them had been associated with some form of Perfectionism for years. Fifty-nine had been involved for five or more years, eighteen for between two and five years, and twenty for less than two years. (No information is available for fourteen people on the list.) Nine of those who had been involved for less than five years were either the dependents of people who had long been interested or young men and women in their early twenties.

The rather scant data on the social and religious backgrounds of these first members suggest no special peculiarities. Most came from rural areas and small towns in New England and New York State. A number of the men were farmers. Others listed their occupations as printer, trapmaker, machinery manufacturer, architect, bookkeeper, shoemaker, and storekeeper. A few had been clerks and teachers, one a lawyer, one a Methodist minister, and one a doctor.

Although there is no church membership data for about one fourth of the people listed (in those days people often attended services of a particular denomination without becoming church members), the religious affiliations of the rest are known: one-third had been Congregationalists and about one-fifth Methodists; eleven had been Baptists and five Presbyterians. From one to three had belonged to each of the following churches: Dutch Reform, Millerite, Unitarian, Quaker, Tobiasite, Universalist, and the Free Church of New Haven.

It is sometimes suggested that converts to unorthodox religious sects have a history of migration from group to group in a constant search for truth. There is no evidence that this was the case with most of the Oneida Perfectionists. Only five persons are reported to have been involved in the Millerite excitement of the early 1840's. Many reported what might seem an unusual amount of thought about religion, but this was not unusual in an era in which revivals were sweeping the country.

All evidence about Oneida's members confirms what someone in the Community wrote in 1853: "the main body of those who have joined the Association at Oneida, are sober, substantial men and women, of good previous character, and position in society." [35]

From the earliest years in Putney to his retirement after the breakup of the Oneida Community, Noyes always insisted that "no sound work can be done in building Communities without very careful selection of material." [36] He invited to Oneida his most loyal disciples from among the groups to which he had been preaching for years. By the end of 1848, eighty-seven adults and children belonged to the Association. Within the next few years about two hundred more persons joined them, earnestly seeking the perfection for which John Humphrey Noyes argued so persuasively.

PERSONALITY AND CHARISMA. As a young student Noyes had been haunted by a sense of guilt and sinfulness. When he failed in the impossibly rigorous standards he set himself,

[35] [Oneida Association], *Bible Communism: A Compilation from the Annual Reports and Other Publications of the Oneida Association and Its Branches; Presenting, in Connection with Their History, a Summary View of Their Religious and Social Theories* (Brooklyn, N.Y.: Office of the *Circular,* 1853), p. 22.

[36] "Niagara Journal," Stone Cottage, Clifton, Ontario, MS, copy of a letter to Mrs. Yoder, March 27, 1881. Italics omitted.

he "loathed" himself. He wished for some means whereby, once and for all, he could eliminate sin.[37] Like many in his era he believed that a permanent sense of salvation was attainable for those who actively sought such a state. At Andover, and during his first year at Yale, his efforts to achieve this sense of salvation sometimes brought relief for a few days but always failed eventually. In the period before his avowal of perfection, he made a particularly determined effort to attain salvation. He prayed for it for hours, and he read his Bible with great earnestness. Eventually he became confident that salvation would come to him. While still awaiting God's action he made his announcement of perfection to members of the free church. With the intellectual commitment made, he went home to await the spiritual and emotional realization of perfection.

> I went home with a feeling that I had committed myself irreversibly, and, on my bed that night, I received the baptism which I desired and expected. Three times in quick succession a stream of eternal love gushed through my heart and rolled back again to its source. "Joy unspeakable and full of glory" filled my soul. All fear and doubt and condemnation passed away. I knew that my heart was clean, and that the Father and the Son had come and made it their abode.[38]

After his "confession of salvation from sin" Noyes always told people that he was perfect, but his convictions sometimes faltered; they did so, for instance, a few months later during his unhappy experiences in New York City. However, in preaching Perfectionism he had found a per-

[37] John Humphrey Noyes's diary, quoted in George Wallingford Noyes, ed., *Religious Experience of John Humphrey Noyes, Founder of the Oneida Community* (New York: Macmillan Co., 1923), pp. 42–63 *passim*. In this book and *J. H. N.: Putney Community,* G. W. Noyes edited and compiled material from letters, diaries, other manuscripts, and published sources. To provide continuity, he included his own textual comments throughout each book.

[38] J. H. Noyes, *Confessions,* p. 18.

manent means to ease, if not to cure, his own sense of guilt and sinfulness. In convincing others that he was perfect, he helped to convince himself.

Paralleling this desire for holiness was Noyes's wish to free himself from the external restraints that were the outward societal manifestations of conscience. His attachment to Paul's Epistles and his identification with this leader of the early church illustrate his feelings. Paul had rejected Judaic "legality"; Noyes rejected the contemporary churches' strict discipline and fixed standards of behavior. For him the gospel fixed "the attention on *power* and not on law," [39] and it legitimized his desire to be his own master, ultimately seeking the correct interpretation of God's will within himself. Noyes wanted to be free and to be responsible for himself. All his new ideas and experiments had the object of encouraging man's natural talent to flower.

Throughout Noyes's rebellion against Calvinist religion and puritan morality one senses his continuous struggle with a rigorous conscience and his inability to throw off totally the constraints that once kept his nervous system in a "morbidly excitable" state.[40] Perhaps he clung to his bourgeois attitudes in matters unrelated to religion and sex because these helped to compensate for the guilt his rebellion aroused. He was proud that his father had tutored Daniel Webster at Dartmouth and flattered to discover that the Des Noyers family was mentioned in the Domesday Book.[41] Such family distinctions bolstered his ego. On the other hand he hated scandal and repudiated any Perfectionist group that broke the rules of monogamous marriage without first creating an appropriate social structure. In person and in print he always presented his unorthodox ideas in a dignified, scholarly fashion and generally justified them through some respectable authority—usually that unimpeachable source, the Bible.

Such compensations could not dispel Noyes's uncon-

[39] Barron and Miller, *Home-Talks,* p. 231.
[40] J. H. Noyes, *Confessions,* p. 13.
[41] *Ibid.,* pp. 73, 74.

scious fears of punishment, however, or prevent him from punishing himself. Long after his declaration of freedom from sin he lapsed periodically into days and weeks of anxiety and neurotic fatigue during which he was assailed by doubts and subject to nervous physical disorders. Periods of great vitality and self-confidence followed, at least until the formation of the Oneida Community. Autobiographical and biographical accounts tell us less about his personal experiences and reactions after that time.

Perhaps Noyes's greatest crisis was his "New York experience." His strange behavior there may be explained in part as self-inflicted punishment. His failure to stir the interest of eminent theologians and preachers raised self-doubts about his newly avowed doctrines and about the legitimacy of his proselytizing efforts. In his uncertainties he began to punish himself. Sleeping little, he wandered about all night; eating almost nothing, he preferred "the strongest stimulants, such as cayenne pepper." [42] One of his experiences is described in these terms: "I went through a protracted process of involuntary thought and feeling, which I can describe by no better name than a *spiritual crucifixion*. All the events of Christ's death were vividly pictured in my mind, and by some means realized in my feelings. I went through them not as a spectator, but as a victim. At length came the resurrection, and for a time I was released from suffering." [43] Then, in contradiction to his religious beliefs, he found himself imagining the Second Coming and saw Christ descending "in flaming fire, to take vengeance on the world." [44] He clung to Christ, but even that refuge failed him and he imagined himself to be the devil. "It seemed to me . . . that no human being ever drank so deeply of 'the dregs of the cup of trembling.' " [45] Yet throughout the whole dreadful experience, he periodically received evidence of God's beneficence.

[42] *Ibid.*, p. 44.
[43] *Ibid.*, pp. 37–38.
[44] *Ibid.*, p. 39.
[45] *Ibid.*, p. 45.

I was led gradually on from stage to stage of endurance, enjoying intervals of rest and comfort, and hoping that each attack of the powers of darkness would be the last. . . . Often in the darkest hour, the voice of God would come to my heart, saying, "O thou afflicted, tossed with tempest, and not comforted . . . in righteousness shalt thou be established; thou shalt be far from oppression; for thou shalt not fear; and from terror, for it shall not come nigh thee." The result of all my sufferings was, that when I finally emerged from them I had satisfying consciousness that my life was "fire-proof." I could say, "Hell has done its worst, and yet I live." [46]

In his New York experience Noyes displayed another personality characteristic that was to become more dominant in later years—his inability to take second place to anyone. When no one in New York recognized him as an important religious leader, the neglect proved unbearable. He needed to be a center of attention in order to reassure himself of his divine mission and to justify what he taught and what he wished to be. From that time onward, in print, in person, by biblical argument, and by personal attack, he strove for a central position in the Perfectionist movement.

As a leader Noyes had to appear self-confident and to assert himself over others. In this way, he was able to conceal an "infernal diffidence" [47] that, even in his seventies, he admitted "was always the cramp and torment of my life." [48]

Another unusual feature of Noyes's personality was his inability to commit himself completely to any idea, action, or person. We see this in his enchantment with the principles of progressive development which, to him, justified the "eternal spinning" of his ideas.[49] His thoughts were worked through in a detached way; he held his mind passive and waited until a relevant thought arose. If it grew in clarity and if it gave him particular satisfaction, he concluded that

[46] *Ibid.*

[47] G. W. Noyes, *Religious Experience,* p. 20.

[48] "Niagara Journal," January 14, 1881.

[49] J. H. Noyes, *Confessions,* p. 59.

it had been divinely inspired.[50] But he did not fully commit himself, even to an inspired idea. If it later proved impractical, he changed his mind. At one time this objection to excessive commitment made him warn his followers against too much concentration and exhort them to follow his example. He was (by God's grace) "master of the art of glancing," that is, he refused to give excessive time or devotion to a particular interest, problem, or person.[51]

The same lack of commitment characterized his personal relationships. He never established close ties with men or women. He insisted that everyone at Oneida should love *all* others, as he did, and transfer attention from one to another in a condition of "perpetual courtship." If this courtship led a man to love one particular woman, Noyes, despite a full record of intense though brief attachments, denied the love, saying, "You do not love her, you love happiness." [52] At Oneida he ruled out the opportunity for complete involvement even in sexual relations by the practice termed "male continence."

In spite of the apparent authority with which he acted, Noyes frequently withdrew from what he had done. Two years after founding Oneida he left to lead a New York City branch community which operated the Perfectionist press. From there he wrote that, although he had founded Oneida and contributed labor and capital to it, he was presently concerned with other duties and assumed "no such care over it or responsibility for it, as would exclude the

[50] Letter from T[heodore] R. Noyes to Anita Newcomb McGee, September 13, 1891, p. 4.

[51] Barron and Miller, *Home-Talks,* p. 96.

[52] *Ibid.,* p. 150. Italics and capitals have been omitted. Some readers might speculate that Noyes found Abigail Merwin's loss so traumatic that he would never again risk the deep hurt of being rejected by someone he loved. There may be some truth in this, but we should notice that, even before he met Abigail, Noyes had established the pattern of incomplete commitment throughout his intellectual life and in his actions. It appears, therefore, that this personality characteristic had some other cause or set of causes that existed before Noyes ever met her.

sovereignty of God or the responsibility of its members." [53] A few years later he assumed more direct responsibility for the Community, but he never settled there for long. He moved back and forth, from New York to Oneida to the branch community at Wallingford. Nowhere was home.

In one important particular Noyes covered his ground so that he could always retreat if the Community failed. In apparent opposition to his teachings of the evils of monogamy, he arranged marriages between many of his young converts. These marriages gave the members the security of having spouses in the event that the Community disbanded. Thus Noyes would not be responsible for casting into a hostile world unmarried men and women who had lived under the system of complex marriage.

In the face of difficult situations Noyes habitually retreated, as demonstrated by his flight in 1847 from Putney to New York City. Perhaps, as he said, his departure was a reasoned attempt to lessen the townspeople's anger. Yet even his loyal sister, who remained behind, chided him gently: "We must laugh at you a little for getting out of scrapes, but you have apostolic example. I opened the Testament last evening to this verse: 'And then immediately the brethren sent away Paul to go as it were to the sea; but Silas and Timotheus abode there still.' " [54] Noyes fled again shortly before the breakup of Oneida; a severe threat to the solidarity of the established Community prompted his hasty departure for Canada.

Any serious failure awakened in him the conflict between his desire for self-expression and the fear of retaliation. He would retreat and then efface his failure by making one of his "eternal spins" and absorbing himself in other pursuits. After all, he could tell himself, Perfectionism was a progressive matter. Each retreat was followed by a new burst of energy and a new venture. For example, as soon as he had fled from Putney, he began to make plans for a

[53] [John Humphrey Noyes], "Brooklyn and Oneida," *Circular,* I, no. 2, November 16, 1851, 6.

[54] G. W. Noyes, *J. H. N.: Putney Community,* p. 309.

new community to be established either in New York City or among a second group of Perfectionists at Oneida.

Despite all his personal anxieties and his failure to become the ideal man he aspired to be, Noyes showed a strength of character, an intellectual scope, an optimism, and an intrepidity that fascinated his followers and convinced them that he was Christ's representative. Noyes was highly intelligent, energetic, and attractive. His features were strong and well formed. He carried himself with a dignified aloofness. As his talks to his devoted followers showed, he could comment extemporaneously on a vast number of subjects, always producing some new point of view for them to consider. To them, even his chronically feeble voice seemed a distinction rather than a handicap.

Much has been made of Noyes's sexual appeal to the women of the Community. A letter written by one of these women illustrates the strength of that appeal:

> Last evening there was a call for volunteers to give a little extra help in the trap-shop, at putting together traps; and as I *used* to work at that, I thought I would volunteer. . . . My work—the noises and the odors of the shop,—everything around me—reminded me of old times; and when not looking up, I could almost imagine that you were standing at the bench with me. And so my thoughts went gliding down the gulf of time, and I saw myself at your side, heating springs for you to hammer out, a girl of fifteen just waking up to the idea that this world contained many things not dreamed of at the children's house. Then I found myself weighing steel for you, and could see your every attention to detail, and myself grown a little older, having just launched out in the great ship of experience, and met one or two icebergs; confiding in you for guidance, yet wayward and thoughtless. Again, the trap-shop was enlarged, and you and I were putting together traps with the greatest zest. I could see you screwing the posts so carefully, and inventing little improvements until we reached the maximum of speed. With every little improvement and incident in the trap-shop, my own life seemed intertwined; for thinking of one brought up the other; and at this stage, I could see myself wild with youthful excitement—having seen the end of several flirtations, but

under new fascinations, and still clinging to you as my guide and refuge. And with this reminiscence, I was truly astonished at your patience with me. I cannot imagine what encouraged you to hold on to me, for I was indeed very wayward, but God alone put it into your heart. . . . My thoughts ran on. I passed through all the incidents previous to Ormond's birth [Ormond was the son of Abram Burt], and saw that as I ended off my education in the trap-shop, I entered (how joyfully you know) upon a new sphere and a new series of lessons—the glad and sober experience of a mother. And by the time I had completed our work I realized, more than ever before, the great transition I then made from volatile girlhood to earnest womanhood. . . . After I graduated from the trap-shop, and God had given me a child, you weaned me off and sent me forth to take care of myself. Do not think of me as sentimental; but I had such a vivid sense of all the past, that I wanted to see you very much indeed, for a little while. So the next best was to write to you. . . . I confess my union with you in everything.[55]

Sexual attraction was by no means Noyes's only appeal, however. The women of his family and the men of the Community were also convinced that he brought a new gospel.

The Community members held Noyes in awe. Because no one really knew him, each could imagine that the leader satisfied his personal conception of the ideal man. In addition to his being away for long periods at a stretch, he spent much time alone when at Oneida. He was aloof and serious. Except for making an occasional pun he had no sense of humor. He demanded complete obedience, yet he refused to assume full responsibility for others: "If the seeds that I sow in your minds ever germinate and grow, it will be because you find, each one for himself, actual communication with God.[56] He fascinated his followers by making them feel that they were almost, but not quite, accepted.

[55] Quoted in Robert Allerton Parker, *A Yankee Saint: John Humphrey Noyes and the Oneida Community* (New York: G. P. Putnam's Sons, 1935), p. 258.
[56] Barron and Miller, *Home-Talks,* p. 288.

They thought that if they continued to obey and to follow his principles, he would eventually accept them.

Noyes's doctrines were too radical for most, but the few persons who were seriously attracted by Perfectionism were taught by a man capable of inspiring the utmost devotion.

II
The Practice of Perfection

CREATION OF A SOUND ECONOMIC BASE. No one would pretend that, in its early years, Oneida attracted members on the basis of the physical comforts of the Community's life. The *Perfectionist* advised those writing for information that Oneida offered few material luxuries. Yet some refused to be deterred by reports of dining on greens and cocoa or doing without butter. Throughly imbued with Perfectionist ideals, they came to join the charter members in their isolated Community. There the first wooden Mansion House, built to hold more than fifty people, amazed the neighboring settlers in their log cabins. How did the Perfectionists expect to feed themselves?

Noyes knew that Oneida had to exploit the resources of its land to become self-supporting. From among the ranks of enthusiastic Perfectionists, he had carefully selected those who were deeply committed to his teachings and also were responsible, talented craftsmen and farmers. They could provide for almost all of life's material necessities in the mill, the smithy, the shoe shop, the farm, the laundry, and all the Community's various departments.

Practical skills and spiritual devotion were not the only contributions the utopians made. They also brought their savings. Few arrived empty-handed; one suspects that Noyes shrewdly selected at least some of them for their wealth. By 1857 the members had invested almost $108,000 in the Com-

Children lived in a separate house immediately adjacent to and slightly in front of the wooden Mansion House.

Oneida Association, Bible Communism (*Office of the* Circular)

munity and its branches.[1] Without this large capital investment Oneida would almost certainly have perished, as did such little-known New York experiments as the Bloomfield Association, the Ontario Union, the Moorhouse Union, and the Jefferson County Phalanx. Oneida could afford to let ten years pass and $40,000 in capital be drained away before the Community began to show a profit.[2]

The Perfectionists soon discovered that farming did not realize sufficient income. The failure was not for lack of qualified men, since a number of the members were farmers by occupation. Henry Thacker, head of the "horticulture department," later won many prizes in New York State agricultural fairs for the Community, but his talents, like the three thousand young fruit trees he contributed, did not benefit Oneida financially for many years. Fortunately for the Community Noyes's brother-in-law, John R. Miller, proposed extending Oneida's economic base from farming to commercial enterprise. Noyes agreed. He believed the Community could keep its unique social organization and still succeed in the American business world.

Ventures into business had to be carefully contrived and executed. This was Miller's great contribution. He saw that settlers in central and western New York State were dependent upon itinerant merchants for many of the commodities available in eastern towns. The Community had had experience in operating the Putney store and had already established another one at Oneida. Miller decided to cover more of the widely scattered market. Oneida would preserve fruits and vegetables grown on its farm and sell them to those who wanted to vary the long winter's monotonous diet. It would manufacture and distribute traveling bags. It would buy in the east quantities of sewing silks, pins, needles, and notions of all sorts and peddle them in the local towns and villages.

Miller died in 1854, a weary martyr to the cause. All

[1] *Handbook of the Oneida Community, 1875* (Oneida, N.Y.: Office of the *Oneida Circular,* [1875]), p. 15.
[2] *Ibid.*

his efforts had failed to stop the Community from losing money. Although profits had increased, they had not yet equaled Oneida's mounting expenses.

Oneida was expected to contribute to the support of five small branch communities which Noyes had established. Of these, the Wallingford Community, in Connecticut, was the only one that survived for many years. Founded in 1851, it contained eighteen members by 1853. As was usual in the branch communities, the land it occupied had belonged to one of the members. It was an attractive site for a Community house, a little distance from Wallingford, on a bluff overlooking the Quinnipiac River. In those early years Wallingford was primarily a farming community. A similar, smaller communal operation existed in Cambridge, Vermont, where Noyes had long cultivated a loyal following. Four years after leaving Putney, Noyes sent a few followers back there to re-establish a communal association in the houses belonging to him, his brother, and his sisters. In 1852, he helped fifteen loyalists to found a community in Newark, New Jersey, where they operated a light-machinery factory that had been contributed by William R. Inslee. This was one of the few branch communities that consistently made a profit. It contributed all its spare cash to a general fund that was used to help offset the losses sustained by the other branches of the Oneida Association.

The branch community in New York City was the most serious drain upon the Perfectionists' joint financial resources. Noyes had moved there with a few Perfectionists several years after the founding of Oneida. He was still anxious to have his views accepted by people outside his communities, and feeling less vulnerable in print than on the lecture platform, where his weak voice had become a distinct drawback, he established a new printing operation. A fire had partly destroyed the old press that had been transferred from Putney to Oneida, but Noyes set up a new one in a house in Willow Place, Brooklyn, donated by Abram C. Smith. With the help of twenty-six men and women from Oneida, Noyes was again able to preach Perfectionism to the world at large.

Most of the other communities could scarcely support themselves, let alone send provisions and money to sustain the New York group and its expensive publications. After Miller's death Noyes realized that he was attempting to do too much and resolved on a policy of retrenchment and concentration. The smaller groups had to be sacrificed to Oneida and Wallingford. Their members were moved into the larger centers and the period of expansion was brought to a close. Not even the two remaining communities were to be enlarged significantly. For the next twenty-five years Oneida maintained a membership of approximately 250, including children, and Wallingford accommodated the remaining 40 or 50 members of the Oneida Association.[3]

Oneida finally became solvent after it had established itself in industry. It did this with the aid of Sewell Newhouse, who in 1848 had come to the Community from the nearby village of Oneida Castle. For years before joining Oneida, Newhouse had made and sold animal traps with springs tempered according to a special process that he had invented. The traps were very popular locally, and orders for them followed Newhouse to Oneida, where he steadily continued to manufacture them. When the demand increased, other Community members joined in the work, and by the mid-1850's, the trap industry was flourishing. Soon

[3] Membership of the Oneida and Wallingford Communities by selected years, 1849–80:

	1849	1853	1856	1866	1871	1875
Oneida	87	130	180	209	225	253
Wallingford		17	?	45	45	45
Total in 1880						288

The proportion of men to women changed little. In any age group there were almost always a few more women than men.

it became the Community's main source of income. In addition, Oneida canned fruits and vegetables and manufactured traveling bags, chains, and less important items like brooms and rustic seats. In the mid-1860's, three Community members were sent to Connecticut to learn how to manufacture silk thread, and with the benefit of their experience another profitable business was established. Of all Oneida's products, however, the Newhouse trap remained the most important. Neither Noyes nor anyone else in the Community seemed disturbed that their perfect society depended for its living upon such a cruel instrument.

As this business acumen resulted in increased prosperity, the Community began to employ workers from the surrounding area. By 1862 some of the less attractive work was being done by these outsiders. Eventually, almost every department hired local people to help with menial tasks. At periods of peak demand Oneida had a supply of temporary workers in the local townspeople and settlers who could help fill a rush order for traps or prepare farm produce for canning. By 1875, in a busy period, as many as 200 outsiders were employed by the Community. Eventually Oneida became a substantial industrial center: in 1864 the net worth of the Oneida and Wallingford property was estimated at $185,000;[4] in 1875 the value was set at more than $500,000;[5] and in 1880 it was $600,000.[6]

Growing prosperity did more than lessen the Perfectionist's work load. After years of sacrifice to the Community cause, the members found that their contribution to Perfectionism brought a fairly comfortable living and, eventually, touches of luxury. In the early 1860's Oneida started to build a brick Mansion House to replace the old wooden building. It was begun on a magnificent scale, and a series

[4] "Record," a manuscript record of daily events at the Oneida Community, from January 1, 1863, to September 15, 1864. May 23, 1864.

[5] *Handbook, 1875*, p. 15.

[6] Robert Allerton Parker, *A Yankee Saint: John Humphrey Noyes and the Oneida Community* (New York: G. P. Putnam's Sons, 1935), p. 289.

of additions over succeeding years increased its grandeur. Sections of two, three, and four stories were added piecemeal, until the Victorian Gothic structure sprawled around a quadrangle. Situated on a slight rise, with its profile embellished by two turrets, the house was admired by every visitor and passer-by. Its adjacent lawns were landscaped with an imaginative selection of trees. Today, one hundred years later, these provide a magnificent setting for the aging Mansion House.

In keeping with the emphasis on the community over the individual, the Mansion's public rooms were far more elaborate than the members' private and semi-private ones. Visitors were impressed by the library's modern decor and its shelves of carefully selected books. They were shown the several communal sitting rooms which were comfortably furnished centers of Community social life. The second-floor sitting room was especially attractive because of its full-length windows overlooking the front lawns that sloped down to the vineyard. Beside it was the big hall. Although it could accommodate many more than the 250 residents, it had an appealing intimacy. It was almost square, with a tiered balcony along three sides and a large stage on the fourth. The wooden benches and assorted chairs on the main floor could easily be moved when the space was needed for dances or games.

In accordance with Noyes's dictum that the individual should rise above selfish interests, no one was allowed much in the way of personal indulgences such as decoration for his tiny room or for his dress. Throughout the history of the old Community, all but a very few older women kept their hair short and wore simple dresses that were styled in the fashion of the times but had skirts ending a few inches below the knee; the legs were covered by practical, loose, trouser-like pantalets. Once the Community had become prosperous, however, Noyes did not disapprove of communal indulgences. The Perfectionists eventually enjoyed a Turkish bath, a photographic studio, a "chemical laboratory," elaborate properties for theatrical perform-

Community women cut their hair short and wore simple calf-length dresses because they found excessive grooming and restrictive clothing unnecessary inconveniences.

Pierrepont B. Noyes, My Father's House: An Oneida Boyhood (*Farrar & Rinehart, Inc.*)

ances, and musical instruments for the orchestra. They even built a two-story house to use as a summer cottage several miles away on the edge of Oneida Lake.

DAILY LIFE AS AN EXPRESSION OF RELIGION. The Community members did not need to wait for economic security before they set about achieving social perfection. Even in the early years, when their financial situation was uncertain, members were confident of the success of Oneida's utopian features. Noyes was determined that religion should remain the center of attention and insisted that it should dictate the whole of Community life. As he put it, Oneida did not "call people away from their homes and employments to attend to religion," but turned "their very arrangements for getting a living into the essential conditions of a school and a church." [7]

If one considers formal ritual evidence of religiousness, then Oneida was not religious at all. There were no regular meetings for services or prayers, and after the earliest years, even Sunday received no particular recognition, except that it was not a regular work day. The Community made every day sacred, not just Sunday. Neither on the Sabbath nor at any other time did the members recite set prayers or hold formal services. Christmas was scarcely recognized as a religious festival. Baptism was unnecessary, for he "that receives Christ by faith, is baptized with the Holy Ghost." [8] Death was no occasion for dramatic display; instead, at a simple ceremony in the hall, people commented at will on the deceased's life, pointing out how he had achieved the objectives for which they all strove. Sometimes the Community members underplayed death so

[7] Quoted in G[eorge] W[allingford] Noyes, "Episodes in the Life of John Humphrey Noyes," *Community Quadrangle,* II, no. 6, December, 1927, 6.

[8] John H[umphrey] Noyes, *The Berean: A Manual for the Help of Those who Seek the Faith of the Primitive Church* (Putney, Vt.: Office of the *Spiritual Magazine,* 1847), p. 430. Italics omitted.

much that they seemed almost heartless. After a funeral in 1868, one member commented favorably on how everyone had "appeared cheerful and light-hearted" and had made "the whole thing . . . more like a picnic than a burial." [9] Such behavior was in accord with Noyes's teaching that, for the Perfectionist, death is only a transitional state and that life after death is very similar to life on earth. In addition, by treating death lightly the Community prepared for the time when Oneida would be a true representation of heaven on earth and when there would be no death.

The one anniversary that, for a while, merited attention was February 20, the day when, in 1834, Noyes first realized his salvation from sin. It was a time of quiet festivities. There were dinners with speeches and toasts to "Perfectionism," "Salvation from Sin," "The Past Twenty-Two Years—Years of Victory, of Hope and of Promise," followed by a dance and even by the exchange of presents. In 1864, the children celebrated the occasion by decorating a fir tree and calling it a Christmas tree. For some years Community members took bread and wine on "the Twentieth," but they attached little significance to the ritual because they maintained that every meal should be treated as the Lord's Supper. By the end of the 1860's the anniversary of February 20 was, according to the *Circular,* celebrated with less formality, and in later years it was not mentioned at all.

Oneida's nearest approach to collective prayer and religious ritual was the continuation of the Putney practice of meeting each evening at eight o'clock. Members gathered informally in the big hall, the women often sitting at the tables so that they could sew in the lamplight. Noyes generally used part of the time to instruct his followers. One member would take down his words stenographically so that, when relevant, these "home talks" could be printed for a more general readership.

Sometimes Noyes prepared his talks beforehand; at other times he delivered them impromptu, inspired by the

[9] "Evening Meeting," *O. C. Daily,* V, no. 68, March 21, 1868, 261.

evening's discussion. He often elaborated Perfectionist theology, but more frequently he would discuss how that theology applied to everyday living. For example, in speaking about "improvement of character," he reminded members of their commitment to self-improvement and told them that although "the idea prevails generally in the world, that character cannot be radically changed . . . the whole theory of Christianity is based on the assumption that character can be improved, yea, radically changed." [10] It was, therefore, possible to bring their behavior into line with their professed state of inner perfection.

On other occasions Noyes made only brief comments. He observed that those who fell sick were often the unspiritual or the weak-spirited among the Community members. He criticized the men in the trapshop for neglecting their spiritual growth in their efforts to increase production. When the mothers paid too much attention to their children, he censured them for showing "exclusive love." At one time he decided that the Community women thought too much about the accouterments bought with their small annual allotment for personal necessities. They must learn, he said, to conquer the "dress spirit," and he insisted that they hand over to him all their brooches as an exercise in self-denial.[11]

When Noyes was absent, a previous home talk was generally read by one of the spiritually superior "central members" who ran the Community under Noyes's general direction. The Perfectionists then discussed and endorsed Noyes's ideas. The rest of the meeting was not hampered by "legality," that is, set procedure. Members heard letters from sympathizers or prospective recruits read aloud and evaluated their writers' sincerity and spirituality; they listened to someone reading newspaper extracts; they discussed their relations with the local outsiders.

[10] Alfred Barron and George Noyes Miller, eds., *Home-Talks by John Humphrey Noyes* (Oneida, N.Y.: Oneida Community, 1875), p. 139.

[11] Corinna Ackley Noyes, *The Days of My Youth* (Kenwood, N.Y.: By the author, 1960), p. 73.

The numerous committees that contributed to the Community's smooth operation presented their reports at these meetings. The more temporary committees recounted their efforts to buy a local farm or a new piano, to organize "butternut picking" parties, or to transport hired workers to the Community factories. Committees from the established commercial departments discussed their affairs at frequent business meetings and announced their plans at the evening meeting. Sometimes they decided that a business decision should be ratified by the whole Community. For example, at a business meeting in 1863, the opening of a sales agency in New York City was proposed, "but there being not a very large attendance & some objections being raised, the decision of it was postponed till the General Meeting at eight o'clock."[12] At that time the Community decided to go ahead with the plan. The agency was established at 335 Broadway and remained in operation until 1868, when, in response to a poor financial report in January of that year, the Community decided to reduce the scope of its operations.

The evening discussions sometimes involved explicit conflict between Perfectionist ideals and material interests. In 1864, when the Community needed more workers, members wondered "whether our business was not such that it was best" for young men and some other members who divided their time between work and study "to forego this privilege for the remaining part of this season." They postponed any decision until the next meeting to give members "an opportunity to reflect" on the problem.[13] In this case they finally decided to give business interests precedence over the ideal of improving the mind and spirit. Their decision was consistent with Perfectionist teaching, for an important part of the interpretation of self-perfection was that the individual should sacrifice for the Community's sake.

The evening meetings did more than remind members

[12] "Record," [July] 23, [1863].
[13] *Ibid.*, [March] 7, [1864].

of their ideals, demonstrate how to practice them, and help to resolve conflicts. When members had participated in discussions, they felt more committed to any decision that was made. It is true that meetings were dominated by an articulate minority and that, despite encouragement, women scarcely contributed. Nonetheless, if a member was particularly concerned about some subject, he could speak out. As long as he argued in terms of Oneida's ideals, his fellow Perfectionists could not dismiss his words without denying the principles upon which their Community was founded.

COMPLEX MARRIAGE. As we have seen, Noyes viewed monogamous marriage as a tyrannical institution that prevented the individual from loving his neighbor. Two people should not "worship and idolize each other." It was "unhealthy and pernicious" for them to become "exclusively attached. . . . The heart should be free to love all the true and worthy," and there should be no form of "selfish love." [14] In the ideal society, monogamous marriage would be abandoned and "complex marriage" would be instituted in its place. At the time of the *Battle-Axe* letter Noyes envisioned this new marriage system as possible only in heaven. Any group which tried to institute the system on earth would face severe social disapproval, and also it would be burdened with large numbers of illegitimate children.

Noyes saw no way of tackling the latter problem until several years after his marriage. His wife had borne five children in succession; all but one were stillborn. Noyes could not accept the common nineteenth-century view that this was woman's lot in life. Weighed down by the sense of his own responsibility, he determined to save his wife future pain and anguish: he learned to practice the system he termed "male continence." Sexual intercourse, Noyes insisted, did not require the final stage of orgasm and ejaculation. The whole process of coitus was, he said, so much at

[14] *Handbook, 1875,* p. 39.

a man's command that he could always stop at any point before an orgasm. Male continence was easy:

> Now we insist that this whole process, up to the very moment of emission, is *voluntary,* entirely under the control of the moral faculty, and *can be stopped at any point.* In other words, the *presence* and the *motions* can be continued or stopped at will, and it is only the final *crisis* of emission that is automatic or uncontrollable. . . . If you say that this is impossible, I answer that I *know* it is possible —nay, that it is easy.[15]

Noyes said that it was especially easy if a man followed his advice about rowing near a waterfall. The nearer one gets to the falls, the more difficult it becomes to return: "If he is willing to learn, experience will teach him the wisdom of confining his excursions to the region of easy rowing, unless he has an object in view [propagation] that is worth the cost of going over the falls."[16] Male continence was natural:

> Every instance of self-denial is an interruption of some natural act. The man who virtuously contents himself with a look at a beautiful woman is conscious of such an interruption. The lover who stops at a kiss denies himself a natural progression. It is an easy, descending grade through all the approaches of sexual love, from the first touch of respectful friendship, to the final complete amalgamation. Must there be no interruption of this natural slide? Brutes, animal or human, tolerate none. Shall their ideas of self-denial prevail? Nay, it is the glory of man to control himself, and the Kingdom of Heaven summons him to self-control in ALL THINGS.[17]
>
> . . . The useless expenditure of seed certainly is not natural. God cannot have designed that men should sow seed by

[15] *Male Continence* (Oneida, N.Y.: Office of the *Oneida Circular,* 1872), pp. 7–8. Some people have suggested that Noyes suddenly found himself unable to attain orgasm in coitus. Since he later fathered ten children in the Community's eugenics experiment, this is unlikely. There is, however, an interesting parallel between his practice of "continence" and his life-long habit of never quite committing himself to ideas, actions, persons.

[16] *Ibid.,* p. 8.

[17] *Ibid.,* pp. 9–10.

the way-side, where they do not expect it to grow, or in the same field where seed has already been sown and is growing; and yet such is the practice of men in ordinary sexual intercourse. They sow seed habitually where they do not *wish* it to grow.[18]

And male continence was healthy:

In the first place, it secures woman from the curses of involuntary and undesirable procreation; and secondly, it stops the drain of life on the part of man.[19]

After Noyes had practiced this "amative" (as opposed to "propagative") intercourse for two years without his wife's becoming pregnant, he decided that male continence was an effective means of birth control. At the same time, he reported, he began to feel that his ideal conception of marriage *could* be instituted on earth. Soon thereafter, he introduced complex marriage in the Putney Community.

Male continence obviously involved such resolution that we may wonder if the men actually practiced it. They did. Those who had, in Community terminology, "upsets" found their sexual encounters curtailed. They learned to exercise self-control or were subject to public disapproval and private rejection.

In practice, the birth control system was effective, if not quite perfect. Between 1848 and 1869, forty-four children were born in the Community. Eight of these had been conceived before their parents joined Oneida, and at least five more conceptions had been sanctioned by the Community. Consequently, at most, thirty-one children were accidentally conceived over a period of twenty-one years.[20]

[18] *Ibid.*, p. 13.

[19] *Ibid.*

[20] Hilda Herrick Noyes and George Wallingford Noyes, "The Oneida Community Experiment in Stirpiculture," Scientific Papers of the Second International Congress of Eugenics, 1921, *Eugenics, Genetics and the Family* (Baltimore: Williams & Wilkins Co., 1923), I, 386. It is possible that not all of these accidents were caused by the men's failure to restrain from ejaculation. William H. Masters and Virginia E. Johnson have recorded, "Frequently

The system of complex marriage would easily have degenerated into license without careful regulation to control competition for the more popular sexual partners and to satisfy those who felt neglected. Noyes said that the members' sexual relationships should be governed by the principle of "ascending fellowship." He believed that the Perfectionists ranged in ascending order from those least to those most nearly perfect. Long before he introduced complex marriage, he had said that those of his followers who wished to improve should associate with their spiritual superiors. The same idea was applied to complex marriage: a person's partners must be higher in the ascending fellowship. Logically this rule could only apply to the less perfect of the two. Noyes realized this and argued that the spiritually superior person would be immune from the influence of his inferior. Descending fellowship, he said, "is identified with the ascending fellowship and gets its authority from it. All true, legitimate descending fellowship carries with it the inspiration of the superior." [21]

In general it was felt that older persons were more advanced in fellowship than younger ones. Thus in sexual encounters it was considered far better for young men and young women to associate with persons of "mature character" and "sound sense" who were well advanced in Perfectionism. In practice, this meant that women past the age of menopause associated with younger, inexperienced men and that unwanted conceptions were thereby avoided. The

---

a preorgasmic secretory emission . . . usually . . . no more than two or three drops . . . escapes involuntarily from the urethral meatus. . . . Frequently, actively motile spermatozoa have been demonstrated in microscopic examinations of this preejaculatory fluid emission. . . . [The fluid] appears most frequently during voluntarily lengthened plateau-phase [coital] experiences. . . . [Such] situations tend to increase both frequency of occurrence and secretory volume of the preejaculatory mucoid material." *Human Sexual Response* (Boston: Little, Brown and Co., 1966), pp. 210–11.

[21] Barron and Miller, *Home-Talks,* pp. 204–5.

system also provided an ingenious solution to the possible lack of partners for the older members.

The women changed partners quite often. One of the few remaining records listing the possible fathers of an accidentally conceived child shows that the mother had intercourse with four men during the month in which the child was conceived. On the basis of the severity of the reproof encountered by someone who showed "exclusive love," it is only to be expected that a woman would have intercourse with a number of different men: probably the number of partners was often more than four a month. The frequency of such encounters varied considerably within the Community. Some persons found themselves very popular; others were in less demand. A physician who interviewed a number of ex-members after the breakup reported that women had intercourse every two to four days.[22] Another report, also by a physician, quoted an obviously discontented older woman who had left the Community. She complained that young girls would be "called upon to have intercourse as often as seven times in a week and oftener." [23]

In the early years the amenities preceding a sexual encounter were simple. A man approached the woman of his choice, and she was supposedly free to accept or refuse his addresses. Beginning in the early 1860's, the request was made through a "third party" who was usually an older woman and a central member. The intermediary's function

[22] Hilda Herrick Noyes, comp., Collection of MSS on the Oneida Community and the Oneida Community, Limited. A full collection of primary documents, the compilation includes, among other items, the findings of a census carried out in 1935 by Dr. Noyes; records of Dr. Anita Newcomb McGee's interviews with ex-members of the Community, August, 1891; and numerous pieces of correspondence, upon which I have drawn extensively in my research. The collection is the property of Mrs. Adèle Noyes Davies, of Toronto, Can. (Hereafter cited as MS Collection.)
[23] Ely van de Warker, "A Gynecological Study of the Oneida Community," *American Journal of Obstetrics and Diseases of Women and Children,* XVII, no. 8, August, 1884, 789.

was, in part, to preserve the Community women from embarrassment, but it was also to check on the members' activities. The Community recorded all encounters,[24] presumably with the help of the third party or, in earlier years, simply with the cooperation of the couples themselves.

Each "interview" required a separate request. If one partner had a single room, as was often the case in later years, the couple could go there. Alternatively, certain rooms were set aside for "social purposes" (the Community euphemism for sexual purposes). At first a couple could remain together all night. Later this was forbidden, supposedly because of the exhausting effects of long-continued intercourse when the man was particularly effective in practicing continence. Probably such separation also helped to prevent the long private conversations that might lead to "exclusive love."

In contrast to the prevailing nineteenth-century view, the Community maintained that sex should be enjoyed, by women as well as by men. Noyes told his followers that "sexual communion differs only by its superior intensity and beauty from other acts of love." [25] He attacked false modesty as he attacked Puritan theology's emphasis upon baseness and sin. Sexual expression was "love in its most natural and beautiful form." [26]

> Sexual shame is factitious and irrational. The moral reform that arises from the sentiment of shame attempts a hopeless war with nature. Its policy is to prevent pruriency by keeping the mind in ignorance of sexual subjects, while nature is constantly thrusting those subjects upon the mind. The only way to elevate love is to clear away the false,

[24] *Ibid.*, 792.

[25] "Abstracts from Pamphlets by Noyes 1848 and 1872," quoted in George Wallingford Noyes, ed., *John Humphrey Noyes: The Putney Community* (Oneida, N.Y.: By the author, 1931), p. 114.

[26] [Oneida Association], *Bible Communism: A Compilation from the Annual Reports and Other Publications of the Oneida Association and Its Branches; Presenting, in Connection with Their History, a Summary View of Their Religious and Social Theories* (Brooklyn, N.Y.: Office of the *Circular*, 1853), p. 31.

Two walls of the balconied sitting room adjacent to the big hall today are lined with doors to what, in the old Community days, were members' private rooms.

Walter D. Edmonds, The First Hundred Years (*Oneida Ltd.*); *photograph by Samuel Chamberlain*

debasing associations that usually crowd around it, and substitute true, beautiful ones.[27]

To be ashamed of the sexual organs, is to be ashamed of God's workmanship . . . of the most perfect instruments of love and unity . . . of the agencies which gave us existence . . . is to be ashamed of the image of the glory of God—the physical symbol of life dwelling in life, which is the mystery of the gospel.[28]

Although visitors to Oneida never reported anything but the most proper behavior and although there is no evidence of sexual orgies, incest, or homosexuality, Community members were undeniably keenly sensitive to the whole question of heterosexual sex. Sensuousness was by no means hidden by Victorian prudery. Noyes discussed sex in his home talks. Reports of the evening meetings refer frequently, if obliquely, to members' sexual encounters and comment on the attractiveness of Community women. The religious, scientific, and descriptive articles in Community publications are strangely juxtaposed with those treating topics like "theories of love" or "sincerity of the passions." Other articles discussed women's dress, the social behavior appropriate to men and women, or men's and women's personalities.

Sexual imagery was common in the religious writings of the time; the Perfectionists, however, used more than most people. An earnest diarist quoted Noyes as saying, "The truth is a living thing and loves to be hugged. . . . Those who hug the spirit of truth will be saved by it and those who flatter it and jilt it will be cast out by its hatred." [29] Mary E. Cragin wrote in her journal:

[The Lord] stirs up my heart from time to time to an appreciation of his mercies, which is as enlivening and satisfying as the reception of new mercies.

[27] "Pamphlet by Noyes Published February 1849," quoted in G. W. Noyes, *J. H. N.: Putney Community*, p. 120.

[28] [Oneida Association], *Bible Communism*, p. 54.

[29] Religious diary, author's name withheld, January 1, [1851]. Italics omitted.

In view of his goodness to me and of his desire that I should let him fill me with himself, I yield and offer myself, to be penetrated by his spirit, and desire that love and gratitude may inspire my heart so that I shall sympathize with his pleasure in the thing, before my personal pleasure begins; knowing that it will increase my capability for happiness.[30]

Because Mrs. Cragin's combination of spirituality and sexual awareness was much admired, after her death in 1851 the Community published the above quotation along with other excerpts from her journal for the edification of its members.

Despite the Perfectionists' determination to make sex an important and enjoyable part of their lives, complex marriage had its disadvantages. We do not know whether the men found male continence one of these disadvantages. The few who wrote about it after the breakup all left favorable accounts, but we have no information about how the majority felt. Whatever these men's reservations, they must have found male continence preferable to abstinence. An objective observer stated, "I have been told by lady members that the practice of male continence . . . was easily followed except by a few men."[31] In the light of modern psychological and biological knowledge, however, it is difficult to believe that the men found the system easy to accept.

Continence of this sort was not required of the women, but although it is known that women were encouraged to enjoy sexual relations, it is not known whether the Community considered a woman's orgasm a desirable consequence of a sexual encounter. However, writing of his "discovery" of male continence, Noyes said that not only was his enjoyment increased but also his "wife's experience was very satisfactory, as it had never been before."[32] Havelock

[30] Harriet H. Noyes, "Mrs. Cragin's Journal," *Circular,* I, no. 7, December 21, 1851, 27.

[31] Van de Warker, *Am. J. Obstet. Dis. Women Child.,* XVII, no. 8, 803.

[32] Parker, *Yankee Saint,* p. 67.

Ellis, basing his account upon correspondence with an ex-member, George Noyes Miller, wrote in 1911:

In intercourse the male inserted his penis into the vagina and retained it there for even an hour without emission, though orgasm took place in the woman. There was usually no emission in the case of the man, even after withdrawal, and he felt no need of emission. The social feeling of the community was a force on the side of this practice, the careless, unskilful men being avoided by women, while the general romantic sentiment of affection for all the women in the community was also a force.[33]

By the Community standards the most serious disadvantage of complex marriage was that couples frequently fell in love with each other. Community reports include frequent criticisms of men and women who failed to suppress one of these "exclusive" or "special" attachments. The rule of ascending fellowship was invoked to prevent young men and women from having sexual relations, in part because they were so likely to fall in love. If it was suspected that a woman refused a man's attentions because of greater love for another, she was severely criticized for lack of the appropriate "public spirit."

In this extract from a diary one can read a woman's earnest prayers for guidance.

Catharine came in and talked some until quite late. I do most sincerely ask for wisdom concerning her case, and myself also. O dear angels I implore for mercy, for help and assistance. It does seem as though I should die alive, and what to do I don't know, but I pray sincerely in the name of Christ, what to do, and I will do it.[34]

A week later she refers again to her own "case":

I thank thee [Lord] for the gift of faith. I love to contemplate and study the subject. Will you please help

[33] Havelock Ellis, *Sex in Relation to Society*, Vol. VI: *Studies in the Psychology of Sex* (Philadelphia: F. A. Davis Co., Publishers, 1911), p. 553.
[34] Religious diary, author's name withheld, January 28, [1854].

me with my relations with Mr. ———. O Lord give me grace in this one thing I do ask in the name of Christ for wisdom.[35]

If an exclusive attachment persisted, one of the offending pair was sent to the branch community at Wallingford until he or she had overcome the worldly impulse. An unfortunate Mr. Delatre was criticized publicly for failing to accept such a separation: "Mrs. Sarah Bradley went to Wallingford for the purpose of getting out of the sort of marriage relation which she had been in with Mr. D. for a long time; but after she left Mr. D. did not want to give her up, & so kept up a correspondence with her"; finally he visited Wallingford, where "he . . . reestablished his old r[e]lations with Mrs. B." [36]

In this case, as in others, Noyes withdrew the sexual privileges of the offenders. In addition, all members knew that such persons were considered less spiritual and therefore lower in the ascending fellowship, which, in turn, limited their choice of sexual partners. In a community that actively encouraged an air of perpetual courtship and where there was an ever-present awareness of sex, this was a particularly serious sanction. Despite the severity of the punishment, love affairs were inevitable. Only continued surveillance could keep them under control and so prevent exclusive love from threatening the communal ideal and the Community's unity.

Close control notwithstanding, clandestine sexual encounters were sometimes arranged, but they "were nearly always confessed and the parties criticised and separated." [37] The emphasis upon public spirit and the disapproval of close friendships between any couple of the same or opposite sexes effectively broke up any nascent group of confidants. The same pressures undoubtedly deterred participants in the sexual act from practicing variations on

[35] *Ibid.*, February 6, [1854].
[36] "Record," [October] 29, [1863].
[37] Van de Warker, *Am. J. Obstet. Dis. Women Child.*, XVII, no. 8, 790.

An outsider's illustration of Community members in the big hall combines the propriety of an evening meeting with suggestive scenes on the stage and in the foreground.

Robert Allerton Parker, A Yankee Saint (*G. P. Putnam's Sons*)

the Community's birth control system. It seems unlikely, for example, that a couple would have agreed privately to the practice of coitus interruptus rather than male continence, for fear one of the parties to the act might later feel compelled to confess. Indeed, a member had no one except the Community to look to for judgment. If he diverged from a Community principle, in all likelihood his deed would be discovered and reported. His alternative was to return to approved practice, confess, and receive a lighter punishment.

EUGENICS: STIRPICULTURE. By the later 1860's Oneida had proved the effectiveness of its birth control system and the practicality of complex marriage. The Community seemed to have reached temporal perfection, but Noyes, who had declared perfection a progressive matter, felt that Oneida was ready for a new stage in its development—an experiment in eugenics. As early as 1848 he had written that "the time will come when involuntary and random procreation will cease, and when scientific combination will be applied to human generation as freely and successfully as it is to . . . animals." [38] In the 1860's he read Darwin's *Origin of Species* and Galton's discussion of the improvement of the human species. His studies confirmed his own ideas. Galton had not yet suggested the term "eugenics," and Noyes invented the word "stirpiculture," deriving it from the Latin *"stirps,"* meaning stock, stem, or root. Eugenics was a venture into the unknown, but by that time the Community was used to such excursions and approached them with supreme confidence.

The members accepted stirpiculture without apparent protest. At the program's inception in 1869, the young men of the Community addressed a statement to Noyes which declared:

The undersigned desire that you may feel that we most heartily sympathize with your purposes in regard to

[38] Parker, *Yankee Saint*, pp. 253–54.

> scientific propagation, and offer ourselves to be used in forming any combinations that might seem to you desirable. We claim no rights. We ask no privileges. We desire to be servants of the truth. With a prayer that the grace of God will help us in this resolution, we are your true soldiers.[39]

The older Community men were considered, on the whole, higher in the ascending fellowship and were therefore likely to be chosen as fathers. Noyes presumably felt that only the younger men who made less eligible fathers need formally acknowledge their willingness to sacrifice their own interests to those of the Community.

The following resolutions were signed by women who were in their early forties or were younger:

> 1. That we do not belong to *ourselves* in any respect, but that we *do* belong first to *God,* and second to Mr. Noyes as God's true representative.
> 2. That we have no rights or personal feelings in regard to child-bearing which shall in the least degree oppose or embarrass him in his choice of scientific combinations.
> 3. That we will put aside all envy, childishness and self-seeking, and rejoice with those who are chosen candidates; that we will, if necessary, become martyrs to science, and cheerfully resign all desire to become mothers, if for any reason Mr. Noyes deem us unfit material for propagation. Above all, we offer ourselves "living sacrifices" to God and true Communism.[40]

The stirpiculture committee, guided by Noyes, rejected anyone it judged unsuitable. Noyes took an extreme Lamarckian stand and selected persons who were well advanced in spiritual development, saying, "Persons must themselves improve, before they can transmit improvement to their offspring." [41] Later, after Noyes had relinquished some of his control to his son Theodore, the new stirpiculture committee paid more attention to the prospective parents'

[39] H. H. Noyes and G. W. Noyes, *Eugenics, Genetics and the Family,* I, 376.
[40] *Ibid.*
[41] Barron and Miller, *Home-Talks,* p. 141.

physical condition. Most participants selected their own mates and applied as couples, but probably about one-fourth of all unions were actually suggested by the committee.[42] The median age of the female participants was thirty years, and the range in their ages was from twenty to forty-two years. The median age of the male participants was forty-one years, and the range in their ages was from twenty-five to sixty-eight years.

During the decade 1869–79, fifty-eight live children were born at Oneida, to a total of forty-four women. Although all are usually classed as stirpiculture children, thirteen were the result of accidental conceptions. Most mothers had only one child, but twelve had two, and two women had three children. Half of the women who had two or three children had conceived one of these accidentally.

The distribution of fathers was less even. John Humphrey Noyes believed sincerely in the superiority of his family line. He sired ten of the "stirpicults"—five boys, four girls, and one stillborn child. His eldest son Theodore, born before the foundation of Oneida, fathered three more. The remainder of the male participants had one or two children.

When they were weaned, the stirpiculture children left their mothers for the wing of the Mansion called the Children's House. After that they saw little of either their mothers or their fathers because the Community feared that frequent visits might lead to special love. The time they spent with their parents varied over the years: at first it was only a couple of hours a week; later it was the greater part of each Sunday.

Before 1869, 135 children had been born at Oneida or had been brought there by their parents. With them the Community had set the pattern for the way in which it reared the stirpicults. All the children under twelve lived in the Children's House. There, in the mid-1870's, 48 of

[42] H. H. Noyes and G. W. Noyes, *Eugenics, Genetics and the Family*, I, 378.

them were being cared for by 3 men and 15 women.[43] They received a regular schooling similar to that of children of prosperous families in the outside world. In addition to doing schoolwork, all but the youngest of them spent an hour or more each day helping on the farm or in one of the Community factories. When they left the Children's House, they continued to work part-time and to go to school part-time. Each evening those under twelve had their own meeting, presided over by the schoolmaster. He read to them from the Bible and from Noyes's home talks, discussed their behavior, delivered criticism, and lectured them on the importance of pleasing God by being good. Indeed, the adults were particularly concerned about the children's spiritual state: they must be unselfish, they must respond to a quarrelsome friend by "turning the other cheek," they must report any backslider, and they must avoid the selfishness of "excessive partiality" or else be separated from their friends. In the 1850's and 1860's a child was reproved severely for even the smallest deviation from these standards. In the 1870's, when the stirpiculture children were being raised, discipline was still strict but not so harsh.

The children did not lack adult attention. There were plenty of men and women to look after them in the Children's House. When they were old enough to feed themselves, they ate at special tables in the Community dining room. Sometimes parents, other relatives, or friends would invite them to eat at the large round tables used by the grownups. At night only a few children stayed in the Children's House. The rest slept in the rooms of adult members. To discourage the growth of special attachments, their sleeping quarters were changed periodically.

Very few of the children have left descriptions of their early experiences. Community accounts describe little more than their daily routines. Therefore, we do not know how the children were affected by the separation from their parents or by the Community's disapproval of emotional

[43] *Handbook, 1875,* p. 20.

attachment to any adults who might have served as substitute parental figures.

It is impossible to assess the results of the stirpiculture experiment. Many of the children were rated as superior and above average by the schoolmaster who taught in the Mansion House school after the breakup. Many went on to college. Some were successful in business, in scholarship, and in the arts. They were healthy, and they lived a long time. But these evidences of mental and physical superiority may be attributed solely to environmental factors. The stirpicults were brought up in a healthy country environment with plenty of fresh air, good food, and attention, and Oneida was isolated from chronic diseases that might have affected children in more crowded areas. As they grew up in the years following the breakup, their families and friends encouraged them to go to college and to achieve worldly success. There is no decisive evidence to support the relative importance of either environmental factors or inherited characteristics. On the basis of the complexity of the whole eugenics question and the small sample size, this is not surprising.

IMPROVEMENT AND EXPERIMENT. Using his belief in progressive improvement as a warrant for change, Noyes led his utopians past the intellectual *cul-de-sac* in which they, like the Old Order Amish, might have been trapped permanently at the stage of the horse and buggy and the hook and eye. He urged the Perfectionists to improve themselves and to improve the Community.

In business, members adopted modern production methods and constantly devised new techniques to increase efficiency. When they were not busy getting out the *Circular,* those operating Oneida's press made labels for the Community's canning business and took on outside printing jobs. Members invented new bookkeeping procedures, a string bean slicer, and a dishwashing machine; the Community purchased one of the recently invented sewing machines.

To reduce the labor of stoking stoves, as well as to increase comfort, steam heating was installed in the Mansion House. When the members in charge of the laundry proved that they got white clothes no cleaner by boiling them, the practice was abandoned.

When they could not avoid monotonous work, members distracted themselves from the tedium. If they held a "bee" to prepare a large quantity of fruit for canning, they would have someone read aloud from a biography of Thomas Jefferson, Captain Marryat's *Jacob Faithful,* or Dickens' *Great Expectations.* After the work was finished, the readings would be continued at convenient times so that those interested could hear the book to its conclusion.

In order to increase all members' satisfaction with their work (and perhaps to create a flexible labor supply) the Community encouraged job rotation. Some people changed positions frequently, whereas others, like the shoemaker, stayed at the same work for years. No one pretended, however, that all were equally suited by inclination or talent for every type of job, and although there was a fair amount of equality of opportunity, there was no equality of attainment. Some people worked only at such menial tasks as helping with the laundry, sewing traveling bags, hammering steel in the trap factory, or working in the silk mill.

Because women participated in this work and because Noyes said they should not be overburdened by excessive childbearing, it is sometimes suggested that Oneida proclaimed the equality of the sexes. Certainly women were not treated as household drudges. The Mansion House, though comfortable enough, was operated as simply as possible; cooked meals, for example, were served only twice a day. Young children spent most of their time in the Children's House in the charge of a few Community members. Before and after school hours, the older children were responsible for such duties as washing dishes and helping to clean out the barns. The mothers, released from maternal responsibilities and from some of the housework, could advance other parts of the Community economy by working in one of the business departments. They were also free to participate in evening meetings, dances, concerts, picnics, and the many varied social activities of the Community.

There was no more attempt to define women as equal to men, however, than there was to assert that all the men were equally talented or equally spiritual. Women were still seen as "feminine" and as possessing very different skills and temperaments from those of men. The *Handbook* of 1875 is quite specific. The Community women had "not ceased to love and honor the truth that 'the man is the head of the woman,' and that woman's highest God-given right is to be 'the glory of man.' " [44] Noyes's principle of ascending fellowship also asserted these differential qualifications and justified differential treatment. "In the fellowship between man and woman, for instance, man is naturally the superior." [45] Thus although Noyes believed that all should have a chance to develop regardless of sex,[46] he was convinced that, even if given equal opportunities, women would do a task less well than men.

Noyes interpreted personal development to include educational attainment. He insisted that all members improve their intellects. For much of the duration of the Community a school was held daily for boys and young men between the ages of fourteen and twenty-six. These and other study groups examined anything from algebra and zoology to phrenology and man's future victory over death. To serve these groups, the Community gradually added to its library; by 1880 it had accumulated over 4,000 volumes. With this stock of knowledge and the help of the few older members who had attended college, Oneida was able to follow the contemporary practice of preparing its own young people for their advanced education. Eventually it sent a dozen or more young men to Yale to acquire

[44] *Ibid.*, p. 26.
[45] Barron and Miller, *Home-Talks,* p. 205.
[46] *Handbook, 1875,* pp. 25–26.

Frank Leslie's Illustrated Newspaper *implies that the Community women at work in the business offices were less industrious than those in traditional jobs in the kitchen.*

Robert Allerton Parker, A Yankee Saint *(G. P. Putnam's Sons)*

scientific knowledge that would be useful to the Community on their return.

In 1866, Noyes said that the Community itself would eventually teach courses at the college level and open its classes to outsiders.[47] Nothing came of the scheme, but Noyes was never troubled by such setbacks. He was always prepared to change his mind and, as in this case, to say that Oneida was not yet ready to take such a step.

Noyes provisionally adopted promising spiritual, scientific, or material innovations. Those that proved successful in practice he kept; the others he quickly rejected. At first, for instance, it had seemed reasonable to him that Perfectionists could triumph over disease. By praying with the sick he and several other members of the Putney Community produced a number of apparently spectacular cures, including that of Mrs. Harriet Hall, who had been both blind and bedridden. Mrs. Hall joined Oneida and survived for many years,[48] but she was never completely cured. Other patients, like children with winter colds, did not respond to prayer or remedial "criticisms." Modifying his earlier statements, Noyes said that the mind could not *yet* triumph over disease, and announced to the Community that it was "to have a Dr. of our own folks, who shall be well established in faith principles & then acquaint himself with all that is good & valuable in the Profession of Medicine." [49] His son Theodore and another young man were sent away for medical training and within a few years were installed as Oneida's physicians.

The Perfectionists were as enterprising in their recreation as they were in their intellectual pursuits and their work. They did not share others' moral or religious scruples against theatricals, dancing, or card playing. Members danced quadrilles and Virginia reels in the Mansion House hall, congratulating themselves if they all followed the principle of ascending fellowship and no couple tried to

[47] "Record," Oct[ober] 3, [1863], and *passim.*
[48] Parker, *Yankee Saint,* pp. 128–29.
[49] "Record," [October] 30, [1863].

dance "exclusively" together. Then it could be said that "a good spirit prevailed." In later years they formed an orchestra and a theatrical group, and the local people made an enthusiastic audience. When the Community presented a program on Christmas night, 1867, "strangers" crowded out the members, but few Perfectionists minded because the performance was part of their general effort to keep the local people's good will. To open the festive occasion, the orchestra played the overture to *Tancredi.* Later, the chorus sang "By the Rivers of Babylon." There were violin, drum, and cornet solos, songs, a scene from *Egmont,* a chorus and tableau from *Il Trovatore,* a farce, and a magician. Afterward the Perfectionists commented that "judging from their outward demonstrations," the outsiders "enjoyed the treat much." [50] Public performances of Gilbert and Sullivan's *H.M.S. Pinafore* and Sheridan's *School for Scandal,* along with concerts and lectures, made the Community in the 1870's a local lyceum.

The members' success in these and other aspects of Community life, combined with their insulation from outsiders' critical interpretations, gave them a sense of security and made them complacent. Consequently, when visitors said that Community women looked younger than their outside contemporaries, the Perfectionists took this to mean that they looked less careworn than other adults rather than that they looked like children because of their short dresses and short hair. A loss of perspective occasionally resulted in behavior that was eccentric, as when they gathered to view the skeleton of Mary Cragin, who had been esteemed for her devotion to Noyes's teaching, her spirituality, and her personal appeal. She had been accidentally drowned in 1851, and in 1868, practical considerations made it appropriate to rebury her remains. Looking at her skull, "all who knew her, recognized the contour—so beautifully feminine. [Her son George] expressed a wish that the skull might be retained. The wish was unanimous. It is to be varnished and preserved." [51] When one considers the fact that members

[50] *O. C. Daily,* IV, no. 151, December 26, 1867, 602.

[51] "Community Journal," *Circular,* V, no. 31, October 19, 1868, 245.

were convinced that they had found the perfect way of life and should continue to elaborate on it, it is surprising that they were not more out of touch with the world around them and more inclined to celebrate and develop their peculiarities.

MUTUAL CRITICISM. In the course of his seminary experiences with a devout group of Andover students, Noyes had discovered the power of personal criticism by companions. He introduced the system, first at Putney and then at Oneida. Any member could be selected or could present himself for criticism by a committee of from six to a dozen persons or, in serious cases, by the whole Community. No regular times were set aside for such sessions, and the number of persons criticized varied according to the individual need and the current enthusiasm of the Community. The comments were often written out in summary form, partly to chart a person's progress and partly to contribute to the detailed written record of all aspects of Oneida's development. Many of the criticisms were published in Community pamphlets and periodicals. Others remain in manuscript. A member's faults and virtues were systematically exposed with relentless candor. One man was, for example, "criticised for lack of religious & intellectual cultivation[,] hardness of spirit, insubordination & independence &c., commended for loyalty, readiness to take hold of anything that needs to be done, good natural qualifications for business, & for having improved during the past year." [52] A criticism of a lighthearted young woman found her

> remarkably outspoken and impulsive, and so her faults are decided and well known. She is a fine specimen of the vital temperament, has great exuberance of life and animal spirits—would live on laughing and frolic—is ardent in her affections, and lively in her antipathies. . . . The elderly people criticise her for disrespect and inattention. She will fly through a room, on some impulsive errand of

[52] "Record," [March] 26, [1863].

generosity perhaps, leave both doors open, and half knock down any body in her way. . . . She has a touch of vanity, —likes to look in the glass, and plumes herself on her power of charming. She indulges in unfounded antipathies, and whims of taste, while she is likely to be carried out of bounds by her attractions. . . . We must cure her of her coarseness, and teach her to be gay without being rude, and respectful without being demure.[53]

Generally, criticisms emphasized a person's bad qualities more than his good ones. Only occasionally were comments primarily favorable. One man who had left the Community and then returned was "commended for never having given us any trouble in leaving or while away." Everyone said that he "was cheerful and never grumbled"; they found his comments in the daily meeting "very edifying"; the members of an adult class he had unwillingly agreed to teach judged him a "first rate teacher"; and several people commended him for giving up tobacco. As was often the case, the Community agreed that earlier failings of this member were in "great measure" caused by his association with spiritually inferior members.[54]

Members found it hard to avoid disapproved associations and to keep up the approved sorts of "fellowships," including "social," that is sexual, fellowships. A person might be criticized for complaining about restrictions placed on his choice of sexual partners or for showing the forbidden but constantly recurring "marriage spirit," "false love," "exclusive love," or "special love." Even death did not spare a member if "the circulation . . . of his private notebook & love letters" proved him guilty of special love and deserving of a "rousing criticism." [55]

Noyes was the only person who was not criticized although he, occasionally, criticized himself; for instance,

[53] [Oneida Association], *Mutual Criticism* (Oneida, N.Y.: Office of the *American Socialist,* 1876), pp. 53–54.

[54] "Evening Meeting," *O.C. Daily,* V, no. 26, January 30, 1868, 101–2.

[55] "Record," [December] 3, [1863].

once, when he had been ill, he said his lack of control had been the cause. However, he did not spare his followers. His judgments were sometimes complimentary, often harsh, and always penetrating. That the members did not rebel against this dogmatic treatment attests to the devotion which Noyes inspired and to two outstanding features of his leadership. First, Noyes was a very good judge of character. He picked out members' faults and strengths with consummate skill. He saw and understood more about them than they knew about themselves. Second, he always judged them in terms of Perfectionist ideals. Thus they could not reject his comments without at the same time rejecting their religion and their whole way of life.

Receiving criticism, especially from Noyes, could be a crushing experience. A member might emerge from it with his ego bruised and his self-complacency shattered. One applicant for membership who did not join but remained sympathetic wrote of his response to the ordeal:

> Here was I who had been doing my utmost to lead a right kind of life; had been a labourer in churches, in religious meetings, in Sunday and Ragged Schools,[56] had always stood ready to empty my pockets to the needy, and more than anybody else had been instrumental in improving the New York Y.M.C.A.—I, who for months had been shaping my conduct and ideas into form, as I thought, to match the requirements of the Oneida Community, was shaken from centre to circumference. Every trait of my character that I took any pride or comfort in seemed to be cruelly discounted; and after, as it were, being turned inside out and throughly inspected, I was, metaphorically, stood upon my head, and allowed to drain till all the self-righteousness had dripped out of me. John H. Noyes wound up the criticism, and said many kind things. I don't know what they were. Perhaps it was only the way in which he said them. Perhaps it was only his personal magnetism or the magnetism of the spirit which he represented. But there was

[56] One of the free schools established in the early nineteenth century by John Pounds for destitute English children and, later, in the United States, for children of English descent.

not a word or a thought of retort left in me. I felt like pouring out my soul in tears, but there was too much pride left in me yet to make an exhibition of myself. The work had only been begun. For days and weeks after I found myself recalling various passages of my criticism and reviewing them in a new light; the more I pondered, the more convinced I became of the justice of what at first my spirit had so violently rebelled against. In my subsequent experience with criticism I have invariably found that, in points wherein I thought myself the most abused, I have, on more mature reflection, found the deepest truth. To-day I feel that I would gladly give many years of my life if I could have just one more criticism from John H. Noyes.[57]

Mutual criticism was effective because members' self-esteem depended almost exclusively upon their fellow Perfectionists' approval. They only left the "home domain" occasionally, and they were frowned on for talking too freely with the local outsiders working in the Community businesses. Visits to relatives outside Oneida were rare, and even correspondence was limited. A member's reply to a critical letter would be read aloud to make sure it contained the right sentiments, and further communication with the critic would be discouraged. Because even friendships were prevented by severe criticism of offenders, by the excessively public nature of Community life, and by the constant emphasis on the communal ideal (members even changed their rooms frequently to avoid excessive contact with any group of neighbors), a member had only his private or the Community standards by which to judge his actions.

Having undergone criticism, a member often sealed the evaluation by publicly confessing his failings and resolving to follow his fellow Perfectionists' recommendations for improvement. Often carefully written out beforehand, these confessions were expected to conform exactly to Community beliefs.

[57] Allan Estlake, *The Oneida Community: A Record of an Attempt to Carry out the Principles of Christian Unselfishness and Scientific Race-Improvement* (London: George Redway, 1900), pp. 66–68. Italics omitted.

In the Community's later years much of the members' summer activity centered on the "quadrangle," almost enclosed by the four wings of the Mansion House.

Pierrepont B. Noyes, My Father's House: An Oneida Boyhood (*Farrar & Rinehart, Inc.*)

Mr. Noyes has been a liberator [who has saved me] from the marriage principality. . . . I have never doubted . . . he was inspired by God . . . yet I have been tempted at times [to] think evil of him . . . because I could get no nearer to him . . . but . . . I was not . . . soft hearted enough to get near him. . . . I am thankful for any experience or suffering which tends to soften my heart and make me receptive to the truth, Mr. Noyes, and the ascending fellowship.[58]

Confessions, like criticisms, frequently mentioned exclusive love and the ascending fellowship. Members would say that exclusive love had caused them misery and suffering, or they would pray publicly for a "spirit of humility" that would make them "loyal to the ascending fellowship."

If anyone reacted to criticism with sullen silence or with angry defense, he was reproved again. Stripped of all social support, he found no reassurance until he submitted completely to the Community's judgment. Submission brought Community approval and personal catharsis. Members found confession a "great source of relief," a "spiritual bath" that "cleansed" them of "self loathing." In search of further gratification they sometimes entered into a "course of historical self-criticism" that brought forth "numerous confessions of wrongs in the past," once secret, "perhaps half-forgotten—but necessarily darkening and poisonous to present experience." [59]

Members even confessed faults that had passed unnoticed. Noyes believed that concealment abrogated the ideal of community and encouraged all members to discuss their failures with their spiritual superiors, particularly with him and the central members. He also encouraged people to tell tales, which he saw as a means whereby the communal good and the delinquents' improvement were both insured. Even members' correspondence was not private. We find the *Circular* printing an exchange between a woman at Oneida and her son at Wallingford.

[58] "To the Family," *O.C. Daily,* V, no. 1, January 1, 1868, 1–2.
[59] [Oneida Association], *Mutual Criticism,* p. 71.

The son, who was thinking of leaving the Community, said he would already have done so except for his family; his mother, in return, wrote of her prayers that he would stay. In printing the correspondence, the *Circular* admitted that it was "written only for the most private perusal, and not with the remotest idea that it would ever be read by other eyes." [60] The editors, however, seemed confident that they were right to publish it: like everything else at Oneida, emotions were shared with the whole Community.

SELECTION OF NEW AND SECESSION OF OLD MEMBERS. On the average, 2 or 3 men and 1 or 2 women left, or "seceded," from the Community each year. Since parents generally took their children along with them, the total number of seceders was somewhat higher. Nonetheless, the Community population was remarkably stable. Of the 109 adults who joined in the first two years, at least 84 either died in the Community or lived there until the breakup. The turnover was greatest among those who had been at Oneida a short time. Of the adult seceders, 46 stayed at Oneida a year or less, while the median length of stay of all seceders was between three and four years.[61] Only a few recruits were needed to maintain at 300 the total membership of Oneida and Wallingford.

Many wrote to inquire about joining the Community. Some were scarcely literate, many were in financial need, some sought homes for orphaned children, and others were attracted by "free love." Some had read the Community publications and were genuinely interested in the doctrine of Perfection. They were encouraged to correspond with

[60] "An Oneida Journal," *Circular,* X, no. 45, December 12, 1861, 179.

[61] Those who left after more than four years included men and women of all ages who had spent from four to more than thirty years at Oneida. Almost half the seceders were accompanied by a husband or wife. Twenty-three men and women left temporarily, usually for a year or so, but six of them stayed away for seven or more years.

Noyes and the Community so that they could be criticized by mail and thus learn what sort of behavior was required of members.

Clara Wait, a forty-year-old woman who had visited Oneida and did eventually join the Community, was critized for her leanings toward spiritualism. She wrote to one of the central members:

> I wish to thank you for your faithfulness in showing me my connection with evil principalities, and to tell you that I thank God for so faithful a man as you are to the truth and for the opportunity I have had to become acquainted with you. Through the discrimination I was able to exercise in the light of your criticism and others at Oneida, I was able to judge all my connections with spirits. I have rejected all communications and refused to pay any attention to visions since my return. I am determined to keep my attention fixed upon Christ and to trust wholly in him and the power of his resurrection. I find peace and rest to my spirit in Christ, and through faith I am steadily gaining in health and strength. I believe the devil held power over me by distracting my attention from Christ through hadean spirits. I confess love for you as my instructor in Christ.[62]

To another central member, a woman, she wrote:

> I thank God every day for the Oneida Community, and feel that I am "growing in the knowledge of God and in fellowship with you." I am greatly benefited by reading the Noon Discourses. I pray in faith and receive what I need daily. I confess my love for Christ and the Primitive Church and Paul, and unity with and loyalty to Mr. Noyes and the Community.[63]

Not everyone could accept the Community's plain speaking about character. After receiving a critical letter, one man wrote that he was "surprised and grieved" to find that Oneida was as "despotic and intolerant as any of the churches" and thankful to have had his eyes opened.[64]

[62] *O.C. Daily,* IV, no. 92, October 16, 1867, 365.
[63] *Ibid.,* 365–66.
[64] *Ibid.,* III, no. 154, June 28, 1867, 615.

Even if they were not alienated by the criticism, applicants often had to correspond with the Community and to study Perfectionist belief for months or even years before they were accepted as members. Despite this careful preparation, Oneida sometimes selected people who could not adapt to Community life and left after a trial period that generally lasted from a few months to a year. The Community viewed the departure of seceders complacently, saying such things as, "The Carpenters took quiet leave of us last night at 12 o'clock. They proved rather indigestible—something of a 'dough-ball'—and we feel lighter to have them gone." [65] Mr. Carpenter, in contrast, spoke humbly to the Community before he left. He felt "the most friendly and kind feelings towards" it, and said "he had been very much benefited by his acquaintance [but he] knew he was not qualified to remain." He and his wife thanked members for their kindness.[66] Most seceders presented and signed such a submissive statement, and very few of them went back on it to attack the Community after they had left. Occasionally, members who had been at the Community a long time publicly discussed the idea of leaving. The more hopeful cases were "labored with kindly"; others were encouraged to depart. In 1881, such a man, Charles Guiteau, a highly unstable person and a totally undisciplined member who had left Oneida fifteen years before, at the age of twenty-five, assassinated President Garfield.[67]

Although the Community more or less required many of the seceders to leave, only one, William Mills, refused to go. In February, 1864, the other Perfectionists literally threw him out of the Mansion House. He later brought suit, demanding payment for his seven years' work for

[65] *Ibid.,* V, no. 21, January 24, 1868, 84.
[66] *Ibid.,* 81.
[67] See Charles E. Rosenberg, *The Trial of the Assassin Guiteau: Psychiatry and Law in the Gilded Age* (Chicago: University of Chicago Press, 1968), for a full discussion of Guiteau's life, crime, and trial and an analysis of nineteenth-century interpretations of and reactions to his mental illness.

Oneida. Generally the Community only gave seceders cash or property equal to that which they had originally contributed; those who had brought no material contribution received one hundred dollars and an outfit of clothing.[68] Mills won his case. After that Oneida made all members sign a formal statement agreeing that their work for the Community was balanced by the room and board received and by the education and training they were given.[69] In this way it kept the matter of secession, like all of Community life, a well-ordered affair.

RELATIONSHIPS WITH NEIGHBORING SETTLERS. In the course of the Putney experience, the Perfectionists had learned the extreme importance of cultivating good relations with the local people. Toleration was a necessary condition for their Community's success. When they first arrived in Madison County, they tried to avoid trouble by keeping to themselves, but their neighbors soon heard reports of their sexual practices and reacted angrily. In 1850 residents of Madison County and of the adjacent Oneida County brought independent suits against the Community. They accused its members of being an immoral influence and a public nuisance. In both cases the Perfectionists' orderly conduct, industry, and discrete seclusion saved them from being forced to leave. After hearing what the local people had to say, the Madison County grand jury refused to allow charges to be brought against the Community at that time. Oneida County's grand jury was less easily persuaded. It took the case farther and had the Perfectionists testify about their sexual practices. At this point the Community began to plan how it would disband. However, the Perfectionists' apparent prosperity and their honorable dealings had already won them a few influential friends in the neighborhood. With the help of

[68] *Handbook, 1875,* pp. 28–29. Community practice was about the same in 1853; then they merely returned property contributed. [Oneida Association], *Bible Communism,* p. 12.
[69] "Record," [April] 30, [1864].

behind-the-scenes activities by these outsiders, the case was decided in Oneida's favor.

These court actions were the only legal proceedings that local people took to try to make the Perfectionists leave. As the years passed, most outsiders became increasingly tolerant: the Community's efforts to create a favorable impression succeeded.

After 1850, instead of trying to hide, the Perfectionists opened Oneida to the public. As early as 1853 they commented, "It is very rare that the family is without visitors. Few are the meals they take, unshared with stranger-guests." [70] With fame and fortune arrived a constant stream of visitors. In 1866 about 4,000 people signed the Visitors' Book. After the Midland Railroad, in 1869, opened a branch line with a stop a few hundred yards from the Mansion House, day trips to Oneida became an even more common entertainment. Visitors strolled through the grounds and were escorted through the Community buildings. Some stayed to attend the evening meeting, and a few remained overnight. It was no strain on Oneida's financial resources to entertain these visitors, for they paid for their meals and accommodations. Although visitors preferred coffee to Oneida's "tea," made from dried strawberry leaves, they enjoyed the almost meatless meals. Vegetables, fruits, milk, butter, cheese, and cakes abounded. "Rarely," said a writer in a *New York Tribune* article of 1867, "have I eaten meals so well-cooked, so neat and so good. They equal, to my taste they excel, those at the best hotels." [71] The visitors had to admit that, whatever notions titillated their imaginations, the Perfectionists' general demeanor was superior to that of the other less perfect residents of Madison County. For their part, the Perfectionists learned to expect and even to revel in this attention, like actors always on stage. If their

[70] H. [Harriet H. Noyes?], "Oneida and its Visitors," *Circular,* II, no. 21, January 26, 1853, 82.

[71] *Handbook of the Oneida Community, with a Sketch of its Founder and an Outline of its Constitution and Doctrines* (Wallingford, Conn.: Office of the *Circular,* 1867), p. 4.

Visitors were surprised that the Community men's dress and public behavior were thoroughly conventional.

Pierrepont B. Noyes, My Father's House: An Oneida Boyhood (*Farrar & Rinehart, Inc.*)

performance was popular, did it not attest to the indisputable superiority of their ways?

In the long run the Perfectionists secured local support less by opening the Community to visitors than by contributing substantially to the local economy. They invested money in land, sold their industrial products, and, most important, employed outsiders in their factories.

Oneida soon earned a reputation for fairness and generosity toward its employees. Noyes anticipated, by more than half a century, some of the enlightened labor practices that later gained general acceptance. Working conditions in the Oneida factories were far superior to those in many others; some employees from the town of Oneida, five miles away, received free transportation; others were housed in Community-owned buildings near their work; and generous wages cemented the amiable relationships between the Community and its employees.

Oneida demanded the long hours customary at that time and utilized child labor, but within a nineteenth-century context, it promoted "a spirit of liberality towards [its] workmen and not the spirit of the world which grinds them down and seeks to get all it can from them for the least money."[72] To encourage its young employees, the Community tried experiments such as awarding weekly prizes to boys who worked hard and behaved well. Boots, a cap, a tippet, pocket-knives, and pocket-books were distributed among them.[73] The Perfectionists also believed that they should safeguard the morals of the older girls who worked in the silk mill and lived in the boarding house. They chaperoned the girls when they entertained young men in the parlor on Sunday afternoons.

The Perfectionists believed it was both ethical and strategic to deal fairly with outsiders. They were seriously disturbed when a member drew blood in whipping a particularly disobedient local boy and settled with the boy's

72 "W[illow] P[lace], Oct[ober] 31," *O.C. Daily,* IV, no. 106, November 1, 1867, 424.

73 "W[illow] P[lace], Oct[ober] 24," *O.C. Daily,* IV, no. 100, October 25, 1867, 399.

lawyer as rapidly as possible. They promptly made amends when a neighbor complained that they worked a hired horse longer than had been stipulated in their agreement. They often made opportunities to improve local relations. When the Community was to receive recompense for a legal claim for damages caused by a broken bridge, it handed over its share of the award to an outsider who also had been involved in the accident. The Community meeting "unanimously favored this idea. Charlie has proved himself to be a faithful servant and a staunch friend of the Community." [74] At another time, members proposed to share with the local townspeople the responsibility for an employees' evening school but finally went on with the project alone because of lack of outside enthusiasm. They occasionally loaned books from their library; they contributed to a fire protection company's annual benefit; they gave money for neighborhood improvements and charities; and when a local band visited, they listened to its music and, with an air of *noblesse oblige,* provided refreshments.

During the Civil War the Perfectionists allied themselves with their neighbors and supported the northern cause. Usually the Community took no interest in political events: it believed that no national problems could be solved until the nation "turned to Christ" and followed Oneida's exemplary way of life. Therefore, although Noyes had opposed slavery since he was a young man, he said that Oneida was a more important "battlefront" than the southern states. By accident no one in the Community was drafted: the Mansion House stood at the border of Madison and Oneida Counties, and each county's recruiting officer decided that the Community lay within the jurisdiction of the other. To help their less fortunate neighbors, the Community contributed cash to pay bounties for volunteers, and it helped local men to avoid war service by paying the fees that would exempt them. Maintaining good local relations ultimately meant more to Oneida's leaders than did the Civil War.

[74] *O.C. Daily,* IV, no. 110, November 6, 1867, 438.

DESPOTISM AND DEMOCRACY IN UTOPIA. From Plato's *Republic* through Bellamy's *Looking Backward* to Skinner's *Walden Two,* utopian schemes have been charged with despotism. Some person or group decides what form the ideal society should take and imposes it upon the utopians. Those who conform are rewarded; those who do not are punished.

Oneida was no exception. As we have seen, Noyes always insisted that divine inspiration sanctioned his absolute power, and no one joined the Community without accepting this "theocracy" and confessing his "union with Christ and Mr. Noyes."

The Community itself occasionally discussed the question of despotism and always concluded that, as far as Noyes was concerned, service was perfect freedom:

> Mr. Noyes's influence [made them all free]. Such an influence [could not] be a despotism. . . . If this was a despotism it was a glorious one. . . . Christ was just as much of a despot as this.
>
> The world cried despot to Mr. Noyes, but those . . . who are honest and true call him father and liberator. . . . Love and unity must be genuine and thorough, and free from all man-worship and idolatry, which Mr. Noyes hates when directed toward himself, or any-one else.[75]

Noyes did not try to superintend all of Community life. He outlined the general principles whereby Perfectionism should be practiced at Oneida and left most of the detailed application to the central members. These men and women ran Oneida during the long periods when Noyes lived in Wallingford and when, in the early 1850's and the mid-1860's, he lived in New York City.

Noyes and the central members brought issues before the Community at the daily meeting. Although they encouraged all members to contribute their ideas, these power-

[75] "Evening Meeting," *O.C. Daily,* IV, no. 152, December 27, 1867, 606.

ful figures generally dominated the discussion. The majority merely ratified their conclusions. Yet the central members followed Noyes's directives faithfully: all decisions stemmed from Perfectionist ideals. At one such discussion:

> Mr[.] Woolworth spoke of persons wishing to visit their outside relatives—Said there were at present quite a number wishing to go, and the traveling committee not being able to sympathise with them in it, thought best to refer the case to the family for counsel. Some discussion about it—the result of which was a desire on the part of the community to avoid putting its members under a legal restraint about such things, to exhort them to see to it that they are guided by inspiration and seek to promote the Community or public interest in it.[76]

Without their devotion to Noyes and their willingness to follow his interpretation of Perfectionist ideals, the central members might have exercised their power ruthlessly. Instead they were strict, but for the most part fair.

Sometimes, however, they were too strict. They punished a man who showed special love by moving him into an unpleasant job without first giving him a chance to reform. To prevent couples from becoming too attached, they forbade members to "pair off" at picnics. They were often intolerant toward the sick because Noyes said illness generally showed a bad spirit. One girl who was ill reported being so afraid of punishment that she stayed at her job pretending to be occupied while her contemporaries did her work for her.[77] A Community salesman was required to give up selling and work in the Mansion House kitchen because he chatted at length with his customers and was felt to be entertaining himself at Community expense, although he may well have found that his was the most effective way of promoting sales.[78]

[76] "Record," [July] 24, [1864].

[77] Copy of a memorandum dictated by H[elen] M. Barron to H[ope] E. A[llen], May 24, [19]32.

[78] "Evening Meeting," *O.C. Daily,* V, no. 31, February 5, 1868, 121–22, and *ibid.,* no. 38, February 13, 1868, 149–50.

The central members enjoyed certain advantages because of their position. They exercised power and they commanded respect. They were relatively immune to criticism, at least from those below them in Oneida's hierarchy. The few existing criticisms of central members are largely approving; for example, one man "was criticised, or rather very much commended for loyalty, industry & a good Spirit." [79]

Rank brought privileges. Two central members toured England and later visited Paris. Others made occasional excursions to New York and other cities. (Noyes himself had set a precedent for such trips by visiting London's Great Exhibition in 1851, even though the Community was then undergoing its greatest economic privation.) Central members had most choice in selecting sexual partners because they ranked highest in the ascending fellowship. The Community insisted that no member should be forced to engage in unwanted associations, but lower-ranking women felt obliged to accept advances from the male central members and the lower-ranking men felt obliged to submit requests for interviews with the female central members. Noyes resolved the conflict between the application of ascending fellowship and the freedom to choose sexual partners by pointing out that all members "naturally" would love their spiritual superiors more than those beneath them in fellowship.

Noyes's son Theodore described the ordinary members' response to despotic control. At one time he said that his father's government "sat lightly" upon the Community,[80] but he also wrote that "the more unthinking class [of the members] were always more or less under criticism." [81] The few former members who recorded their opinions of conditions before the breakup concluded that Oneida was a pleasant place to live. Most of them, however, had been members of the central group. While we do not know the feelings of those who did not write about Oneida, they cannot all have

[79] "Record," [January] 31, [1863].
[80] Letter from T[heodore] R. Noyes to Anita Newcomb McGee, September 13, 1891, p. 13.
[81] *Ibid.*, p. 15.

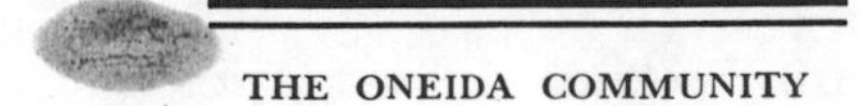

felt dissatisfied, or they would have left. Some who wished to go might have feared that, in the eyes of the world, nothing could restore the reputation of one who had practiced perfection and "free love," but they also knew that others had left and re-established their lives outside. Furthermore, at the breakup, few members wanted to give up either complex marriage or communal living, although many wanted modifications of these institutions. There is no indication that members were seriously dissatisfied with the existing system, and they accepted rule by elite as part of that system.

Two conditions made democratic leadership impossible at Oneida. First, complex marriage, as practiced, depended upon the rule of the ascending fellowship and thus upon very close control by those highest in fellowship, specifically Noyes and the central members. Second, members believed that Noyes was divinely inspired when he taught Perfectionism: from the central members down, all acted in accordance with the idealistic principles derived from his religious system. Whoever asserted his views over Noyes's would be questioning not only Noyes but also the whole justification for Oneida's existence. It was just such a question, in fact, that precipitated the breakup of the Community.

III
The Breakup

Decline of the Original Ideals. By the 1870's, the Perfectionists had been operating their extraordinary social system for more than twenty years and had come to believe they had found the solutions to all social problems. However, in their complacency, they failed to notice the subtle changes that were leading to the breakup of the Community as they had known it.

Perfectionism was changing in character—becoming less religious and more social. The doctrinal elements of Oneida's religion were not in themselves necessary for survival, but the value system that derived from that doctrine *was* necessary. Perfectionist theology had defined and justified the ideals that had guided all of Community life.

Noyes himself led the trend away from religion. Despite the fervor of his earlier religious propensities, in the 1860's he became preoccupied with the then infant study of social science. His efforts in pursuit of his new interests led in 1870 to the publication of his study of American socialisms based on the field work of an outsider, A. J. Macdonald. A few years after Macdonald's last visit to Oneida in 1854 and his subsequent death, Noyes acquired his voluminous notes and structured them into a full treatise on the subject.[1] His con-

[1] *History of American Socialisms* (Philadelphia: J. B. Lippincott & Co., 1870). Macdonald's materials are now in the Yale University Library. They consist of an unsystematic collection of his own notes and others' published and unpublished accounts of the communities.

In the late 1860's, his red hair turning white, John Humphrey Noyes was a distinguished looking man.

George Wallingford Noyes, ed., The Religious Experience of John Humphrey Noyes *(Macmillan Co.)*

tinued biblical studies now inspired his interpretation of society rather than his interpretation of religion. Despite the consistently strong mystical element in his thinking, Noyes often looked to science, not the Bible, to explain and justify social action.

The editorial policies of the Community periodicals reflect his changed concerns. In the 1840's and 1850's the *Witness* and its successors were devoted largely to the explication of Perfectionist theology. As early as 1864 Noyes wrote that the projected "second series" of the *Circular* would be "an 'entertaining' instead of a strictly 'religious' paper," and he warned the "old fogies" in the Community to prepare for "heresies, innovations & novelties." [2] The decisive victory of secularism over religion was signaled by the publication in 1876 of the *American Socialist* in place of the *Oneida Circular*. In introducing the new periodical Noyes omitted all mention of Perfectionism and wrote instead that the paper would "make a faithful public record of facts relating to the progress of Socialism every-where, and . . . offer to Socialists of all kinds a liberal medium of exchange and discussion." [3]

In governing Oneida in the 1850's Noyes had insisted that the members spend several hours a day in religious study, discussion, and contemplation. By 1864 he was encouraging "clubs for mutual improvement" and suggesting that Community members experiment with "how to spend Sunday in a scientific manner" so that, when they formed new communities, they would "know how to put the weeks together." [4] In the 1850's he had strongly disapproved of spiritualism, but by the 1870's he was encouraging his followers to investigate the phenomenon. Some, Theodore Noyes among them, studied the subject extensively, visiting mediums and perusing all available publications. A few,

[2] "Record," a manuscript record of daily events at the Oneida Community, from January 1, 1863, to September 15, 1864. April 9, 1864.

[3] John H. Noyes, William A. Hinds, and F. Wayland-Smith, "Prospectus of a New Weekly Paper Devoted to Socialism," *Oneida Circular,* n.s., XIII, no. 10, March 9, 1876, 73.

[4] "Record," [August] 28, [1864].

not including Theodore, went so far as to declare that they could communicate with the spirit world.

During the 1860's and 1870's, Noyes's physical infirmities made it impossible for him to command as he once had. His perennially weak voice became reduced to a whisper, and his hearing deteriorated. By 1875, although he was only sixty-four, he could no longer hear ordinary conversation, and when he attended the daily meeting, someone had to repeat members' comments to him in a loud voice. He delegated more and more responsibility to the central members and gradually allowed them to govern almost completely without his intervention and advice. The change contributed to the decline in Perfectionist theology and to a shift in the emphasis placed on its ideals. This is not to say that the old beliefs were abandoned: many central members continued to espouse and to try to teach them. Others, eager to restore the predominance of religion to the Community but insensitive in their zeal to the traditional religious practices, wanted to introduce revival meetings and other such customarily unacceptable programs to bring about their ends. Still others tried to adapt the old beliefs in such a way that they would be applicable to a social rather than a religious utopia. Whatever the approach planned to reunite the Community spiritually, Noyes was dissociated from it. Earlier he had kept in constant touch with Oneida, even during his frequent sojourns at Wallingford and elsewhere; by the 1870's he was absent even while present, retiring during evening meetings to the upper sitting room which adjoined the big hall, responding with silence to the issues that he had once interpreted with critical acumen.

Left to their own devices in conducting the affairs of the Community, Noyes's lieutenants, in disagreement about both Community goals and the means by which to achieve them, could hardly have been expected to re-establish the balance and consistency of various aspects of life at Oneida. Instead they created a tension which precluded resolution. While insisting, on the one hand, that self-improvement and self-realization were to be achieved in intellectual terms, they placed increased emphasis, on the other hand, on submission to the communal, that is, the central members', will. The themes of obedience and sacrifice found their way into print as well as practice. The *Handbook* of 1875, eliminating the motif of "confessing Christ as a Savior from sin," said, "We all believe in Christ as a Savior from selfishness." [5] In making unselfishness the major tenet of the system, the leaders destroyed once and for all the balance that had existed between a member's duty to himself and his duty to society.

The Community was threatened, too, by its inability to imbue its young with the spirit of the founders. Since Oneida children, unlike their parents, were members of the Community by virtue of family ties rather than by choice, their appreciation of Community ideals had to be developed. Whether taken to Oneida as children or born there—in 1875 the ratio of these two groups was approximately four to one[6]—the young people were exposed to the Perfectionist value system and its emphasis upon mutual criticism, the providence of God in daily life, and, without its sexual overtones, the principle of ascending fellowship. The message did not fall on deaf ears: as one child related her understanding of the system, "We must get near God, and to those better than we are, who will improve us." [7]

Exposure to the system did not necessarily result in total acceptance of it, however, although there is no evidence that the failure of the religious aspects of Perfectionism to inspire the young was the result of any deliberate rejection on their parts. Rather, unlike their parents, they were not a psychologically select group predisposed to accept the religion; and like their parents, they existed in an atmosphere in which a concern for the Community as a social entity was supplanting the reverence for its original reason for being. It

[5] *Handbook of the Oneida Community, 1875* (Oneida, N.Y.: Office of the *Oneida Circular*, [1875]), p. 29.

[6] These figures, referring to young people over sixteen years of age, do not include the children of the stirpiculture experiment. In 1875 the stirpiculture children were all under six years old.

[7] *O.C. Daily*, III, no. 104, May 2, 1867, 415.

is understandable, then, that the young did not greet Perfectionism with the convert's fervor.

Ironically, it was probably not the Community's inconsistent attitude toward its own religious principles but its consistently strong emphasis on education which allowed children to follow a somewhat different course from that taken by their parents. All children were encouraged to read widely. To the detriment of their devotion to Community ideas, they grew up with an appreciation of literary scholarship, with scientific training, and with at least a vicarious taste of the attractions of the outside world. By the time of the breakup of the Community, at least one-third of the sixty-six people between the ages of twenty-two and thirty-nine had received some form of education beyond that which had been offered at Oneida. It is true that not all were at liberty to pursue their own academic interests. The adults, recognizing that the Community's future professional needs must be met by those being educated at the time, abrogated that part of the ideal of self-perfection urging maximum realization of one's innate potential and advocated instead that young people be educated to fill the special needs of Oneida. In so doing, they introduced an element of disharmony that had not been present in the early Community: once, that which had been in the interest of the individual was simultaneously in the interest of Oneida; now, the individual's interests were to be sacrificed so that the goals of the Community might be achieved. Despite the limitations imposed in the name of the good of the system, however, Oneida's youth faced adulthood with educational backgrounds that were very different from and much broader than those of their parents.

Although it might seem that disillusionment with the Community would have stimulated the young people to make their way elsewhere, the fact is that they seceded from the Community no more frequently than did their elders. Oneida still had much to offer the younger generation although less than even it could have recognized. Whether broadened educational experience or the decline of religion

With prosperity, the Community began a brick building on a slight rise above the wooden Mansion House; by 1878 a lawn covered the site of the Perfectionists' first communal house.

Handbook of the Oneida Community (1867), (*Office of the* Circular)

at Oneida or Community membership by inheritance rather than choice was the principal cause of the failure of the young to embrace Oneida with the zeal that their parents had, the effect was that the Community was to experience the greatest threat to its existence without the benefit of a "spirit of unity."

Despite their lack of the original sense of community, for most of the 1870's the Perfectionists still looked to Noyes for leadership. Yet, as his disabilities worsened, everyone wondered who would be his successor. In 1875, Noyes proposed his thirty-six-year-old son Theodore. His decision illustrated how far Oneida had moved from the old Perfectionist beliefs: for years Theodore had struggled in vain to reconcile himself to his father's religious principles; now Noyes wanted to make him his successor. Perhaps he thought that a Yale graduate in medicine who openly questioned the truth of Perfectionism would be precisely the man to realign the Community's objectives to parallel the changed conditions of a new era. More probably, however, Noyes's belief that his children had inherited his superior qualities blinded him to the problems that an agnostic in command of Oneida would create.

Since for Theodore there was no question of divine mission, as there had been for his father, the matter was put forward for Community consideration. After a great deal of discussion, the proposal was defeated, officially because of objections to Theodore's heterodox theological opinions. Many members recognized, however, that Theodore's abilities did not equal his father's. And Theodore himself did not want the job.[8]

John Humphrey Noyes stayed unwillingly in his post until 1877, when he appointed a committee to govern the Community and placed his son at its head. Despite Theodore's reluctance and the Community's failure to endorse him totally, he managed the material aspects of Community life well enough. Under his leadership a new wing of the

[8] Letter from Theodore R. Noyes to Anita Newcomb McGee, April 15, 1892, p. 4. Manuscript marked "Letter never sent."

Mansion House was begun. At Wallingford he built a factory that used water power to produce tin-plated spoons, but his scheme for industrial expansion was frustrated when, soon after the factory was completed, an epidemic of malaria caused almost all of the Perfectionists then living at Wallingford to return to Oneida.[9] Theodore also headed the twelve-member stirpiculture committee that had been created formally in 1875. There his influence and that of the other physician, George Cragin, accounted for the increased attention paid to prospective parents' physical, as opposed to spiritual, qualities. No activity could subdue Theodore's religious doubts, however, and some of the members could not conceal their objections to his appointment. By the summer of 1878, Theodore reported, he was "so used up in the struggle to agree with father" that he "temporarily" left Oneida for New York City.[10]

The few available reports differ about what happened during the following months. One account says that Theodore had nothing to do with Oneida;[11] another indicates that he continued to rule from a distance, directing the members' lives in minute and exasperating detail.[12] Theodore himself passes over the period and simply says that, on his return in the autumn of 1878, he suffered a severe attack of gallstones which put him out of the running as a successor.[13]

[9] In the 1870's malaria, spread by soldiers returning from the Civil War, was endemic over almost the whole of the United States. Between 1860 and 1900 an epidemic spread through Connecticut and "between 1860 and 1870 the fever spread up the Quinnipiac valley," where the Wallingford Community was located. See James C. Hart, "Malaria—A Post-War Threat," Connecticut State Department of Health, *Monthly Health Bulletin,* May, 1944, p. 2.
[10] Letter from Theodore R. Noyes to Anita Newcomb McGee, April 15, 1892, p. 4.
[11] Robert Allerton Parker, *A Yankee Saint: John Humphrey Noyes and the Oneida Community* (New York: G. P. Putnam's Sons, 1935), p. 278.
[12] Pierrepont [B.] Noyes, *My Father's House: An Oneida Boyhood* (New York: Farrar & Rinehart, Inc., 1937), p. 161.
[13] Letter from Theodore R. Noyes to Anita Newcomb McGee, April 15, 1892, p. 4.

Community members discussed the problem of succession worriedly. Noyes's other adult son, born to Mary Cragin thirty years before, was, by general admission, unsuited for leadership: he had spent a short time in the local insane asylum. No likely candidate appeared.

In the last years of the 1870's the Community was, for the first time, vulnerable to internal dissension. When the leaders failed to promote Perfectionist theology, they had undermined the members' faith in the divine justification for Oneida's way of life. When they failed to implement the original Perfectionist ideals, they had deprived members of common principles on the basis of which to resolve disagreements. The only consistent reinterpretation of the ideals—that giving greater emphasis to personal sacrifice for the Community—had upset the balance that Noyes had achieved earlier in satisfying individual and group interests. Noyes himself was no longer seen as Christ's representative but as the person who "exercises more influence in the affairs of the Community than any-one else because . . . his head is wisest and his heart largest and truest." [14] Unguided and uncertain, the Community members continued their daily lives, outwardly calm but inwardly anxious.

The point of contention which brought into being two opposing parties was the question of the initiation of virgins into the sexual realities of Community life. The initiation of young men posed no problem: sexual relations began routinely for them at puberty. The difficulty arose rather in connection with the young girls. By common consent Noyes had always assumed the responsibility for introducing them to sexual experience. His attraction to them was real, and he developed a strong romantic attachment to each one. His own rule forbidding exclusive love prevented the relationships from lasting very long and preserved him from the disillusion of fading romances. The women, however, continued to love him for years. Noyes established such strong and lasting emotional bonds that, during the breakup, "with scarcely any exception he retained the respect and love of all

[14] *Handbook, 1875*, p. 28.

the young women" [15] as well as of the older women who had come to the Community years earlier.[16]

As he grew older, Noyes sometimes delegated the role of "first husband" to one of the several central men.[17] Early in 1879, two of them questioned Noyes's right to decide who was to introduce young women of the Community to sexual experience. One of these men, William A. Hinds, had been at Oneida since its founding; the other, James W. Towner, had joined in 1874. It is probable that their outspoken protest was precipitated by some personal disappointment over the selection of first husbands. In any event, approximately thirty men and women joined them to form a highly aggressive party protesting Noyes's authority.[18] The schism between the "Townerites" and the "Noyesites" was not one of the young against old, oppressed members against central figures, or religious against non-religious members. Within each of these groups there were those who supported the "Townerites" and those who supported the "Noyesites."

The Towner party held one powerful weapon: not only did Noyes generally act as first husband; he also assumed this responsibility when some of the girls were very young. Documentary evidence for this fact is to be found in Ely van de Warker's gynecological study published in 1884. In

[15] Letter from Theodore R. Noyes to Anita Newcomb McGee, April 15, 1892, p. 3.

[16] *Ibid.*, p. 2.

[17] Noyes may well have felt less interested and less capable of performing the role of first husband, but he was certainly still attracted to women. As his "Niagara Journal" indicates, he could still be emotionally and physically drawn to both a girl of fourteen and a woman of thirty-seven in the months after June, 1879, when he had left Oneida. Observing the standards of the outside world, he made no sexual advances to them. "Niagara Journal," Stone Cottage, Clifton, Ontario, MS, January, 1881 (recollections of Noyes's experiences at Strathroy).

[18] It is sometimes suggested that Towner's followers, almost equally divided between men and women, consisted only of his relatives and friends who had come to Oneida with him. While it is true that most of these did support Towner, more than two-thirds of his followers came from elsewhere in the Community.

the 1870's Theodore Noyes told Dr. van de Warker that there were some fears in the Community that the peculiar sexual practices of the members might have a bad effect on the health of the women. Since there is no indication that any member had reason to fear ill health and since the medical ramifications of complex marriage had not concerned members for thirty years, their fears seem suspect. Perhaps behind them lay unexpressed objections to the management of the system. In any case, in 1877 Dr. van de Warker was invited to examine the women. Within the limitations of medical science of the 1870's and in spite of his expressed objections to complex marriage, he was unable to find any significant differences in the health of the women examined at Oneida and that of those he encountered in his regular practice.[19] His tabulations of personal data for forty-two women do reveal to us, however, that the twenty-three who had begun menstruation at the Community had been introduced to complex marriage very soon after the onset of menstruation. The ages ranged from ten to eighteen years; the average was just over thirteen.[20]

Dr. van de Warker wrote that when he had examined thirty-one "bright and intelligent women . . . modest and lady-like in their manner" and had collected personal data about eleven more, John Humphrey Noyes sent an order to discontinue the proceedings.[21] Thus, van de Warker's report refers only to a non-random sample of about one-third of the Community women who were between the ages of fifteen and eighty. Limited though it was, his investigation provides us with evidence of the serious threat that the Towner fac-

[19] Ely van de Warker, "A Gynecological Study of the Oneida Community," *American Journal of Obstetrics and Diseases of Women and Children,* XVII, no. 8, August, 1884, 796, 803–10.
[20] *Ibid.,* p. 795. The median figure was thirteen years. All but two of the women examined started menstruating between the ages of twelve and fifteen. Van de Warker's tabulation must have been based upon information provided by the women themselves or have been taken from Community records and must, therefore, be accurate.
[21] *Ibid.,* pp. 791, 792.

tion could use against Noyes. If they wished, one or more of their members who had an underage daughter could bring legal action against him and any other central members who had acted as a first husband, accusing them of statutory rape. Obviously, the members of the Noyes party could bring similar suits against men in the Towner party who, although they had not initiated any of the virgins, had had sexual relations with young women below the age of consent. If any legal action or actions were begun, however, Noyes, as originator of complex marriage and as the traditional first husband, would be the man upon whom the outside world would focus its condemnation.

Bitter arguments arose as the Community took sides on the questions of who should authorize a girl's introduction to complex marriage and who in the Community should provide that introduction. The Townerites charged Noyes and his loyal lieutenants with despotism: they received the old reply in defense—Noyes's autocratic rule was justified as the revelation of God's will. But people on both sides had begun to question Noyes's divine mission, and few thought that he was making clear enough the principles for which he, and supposedly they, stood. Dissent focused on Noyes and on the subject of virginity, but it really extended to the whole manner in which the Community was governed.

New troubles were heaped upon the wrangling Community. A group of clergymen led by Professor John W. Mears of nearby Hamilton College threatened an attack upon the "immoral" Perfectionists. The Community had long been accustomed to countering such attacks, but now it could scarcely put up united opposition. On June 22, 1879, Myron Kinsley, one of the men faithful to Noyes, discussed with him the fear (which may or may not have had substance) that hostile Community members or Mears's group, acting alone or in collaboration, might bring criminal action against him.[22] The two men decided that Noyes should

[22] Although Towner and Hinds were equally liable to a charge of statutory rape, the extreme fear Noyes expressed in his account suggests that he believed himself the more vulnerable, perhaps

leave immediately. Stealthily, in the night, his plan known to only one or two persons, he fled some two hundred miles to the international frontier and the safety of Canada.

The opposing parties at Oneida were left to resolve the problem of Community government. It seemed decidedly worth settling, for at that point none anticipated the breakup that was only eighteen months away. To maintain communication with Noyes, Kinsley traveled back and forth between Oneida and Strathroy, where Noyes was enjoying the hospitality of Walter Brett, a non-Community Perfectionist. While it appeared to many in the Community that Kinsley was acting as Noyes's representative, in fact their leader *in absentia* had followed his life-long pattern of turning away from a problem before which he felt powerless and had given Kinsley "*carte blanche* to do what he pleased." [23] As Noyes described his feelings later, "In my heart I laid down my sceptre and lost all desire to rule in the old way. . . . My greatest desire was to get out of it and to clear myself of all care [,] even knowledge of [the Community's] external affairs." [24]

A week after Noyes's departure, Kinsley took to Oneida a proposition, ostensibly from Noyes, suggesting that the disaffected Townerites state their grievances to the Noyes party. The dissidents met and presented their list of complaints and recommendations. The latter included the suggestions that an administrative council be appointed to govern the Community and that the sexual relations of those under age be the concern of the young people and their parents and guardians. Since the Noyes party did not object to these terms, the list was conveyed to Canada for approval. There Noyes went through the formality of agreeing and returned the list in the form of a proposition that met all the basic Townerite demands. The Community voted unanimous agreement, and an administrative council of twelve persons

---

because neither of the other men had been a first husband. See J. H. Noyes, "Niagara Journal," January 2 and 3, [1881].

[23] *Ibid.*, January 6, [1881].

[24] *Ibid.*

representing both sides in the dispute was appointed to govern Oneida.

Despite their differences, neither party wished to discontinue complex marriage. After the administrative council had been appointed, the Community was fully prepared, therefore, to face the forthcoming attack by Professor Mears and his clerical colleagues. As long as all members remained committed to the marriage system, Mears could collect no legal evidence of statutory rape or adultery. Unfortunately, however, the council could not agree on the way to manage complex marriage. Should it be operated as before, based on the principle of ascending fellowship; or should those who felt exploited by the system be given varying degrees of freedom? Should the council sanction stirpiculture unions, none of which had occurred since the latter part of 1878, almost a year earlier? [25]

Theodore Noyes and another council member looked upon themselves as neutral third parties. They, with a few sympathizers in the Community at large, argued for the impracticality of governing complex marriage by committee, insisting, without any specific rationale, that nothing could then prevent the system from degenerating into license. They communicated their fears to Noyes himself. Not realizing the extent to which he had detached himself from Oneida, they were surprised when the exiled leader responded by sending a message proposing exactly what they suggested—that complex marriage be abandoned. After some further exchanges the council accepted the proposition and presented it to the Community in August, 1879. Despite the general sentiment in favor of continuing the system in some revised form, the members realized the impracticality of all their suggested solutions and, with only Hinds abstaining, voted unanimously to bring their sexual venture to an end.

Members were to return to monogamy or celibacy. Quite a number of the older members were already married.

[25] The fact that the stirpiculture experiment persisted throughout so many years of Community disharmony provides further evidence of the members' faith in the permanence of Oneida.

Many of the remainder arranged marriages, generally deciding to confirm the decisions by contract instead of having a local minister officiate.

During these months, Oneida maintained its regular routine, most members thinking the Community would survive. But its social structure had been based upon complex marriage, and the return to monogamy only aggravated its problems. Without faith in Noyes's divine sanction, without a united belief in Perfectionism, and without complex marriage, Oneida lost its justification for existence. It had neither the leaders nor the heart to tackle the drastic reorganization necessary to preserve utopia. Consequently, twelve months after the end of complex marriage, a commission composed mostly of members of the administrative council was assigned the responsibility of supervising an orderly retreat from communalism.[26] If the Community were to be abolished and its holdings sold, the members would lose a large proportion of the $600,000 book value of their properties. Furthermore, the Community members would be flung into a hostile world, bereft of capital and of worldly experience. Alternatively, the commission believed that Oneida could continue to operate its industries on behalf of its members. In the form of a joint-stock company, it could provide employment for those who wanted to work and could pay regular dividends on stock apportioned to each member.

The latter possibility was accepted as the course of action. Oneida would divide indeed, but it would reorganize immediately. The Agreement to Divide and Reorganize was made in September, 1880. Two weeks later, with the dissent of only Sewell Newhouse, the Plan of Division was formally accepted. On January 1, 1881, the Oneida Community was legally transformed into the Oneida Community, Limited.

THE FRAGILITY OF UTOPIA. Because for twenty years the Oneida Community approached Noyes's vision of the ideal

[26] Letter from Theodore R. Noyes to Anita Newcomb McGee, April 15, 1892, p. 5.

At the breakup the Community symbolized its return to monogamy by issuing marriage licenses.

Marriage License.

License is hereby granted to John Homer Barron and Helen C. Miller to join themselves in marriage on the grounds stated in their application dated March 5th

For the Administrative Council,

George D Allen Chairman

Oneida Community, March 12 1880

Pierrepont B. Noyes, My Father's House: An Oneida Boyhood (*Farrar & Rinehart, Inc.*)

society, it is frequently cited as an example of a successful utopia. That it should be so regarded is attributable to a number of factors, all of which have implications for Oneida and for other utopian groups as well. In the principles underlying its philosophy, the quality of its leadership, and the make-up of its membership, Oneida provides clues which enable us to understand something of a utopia's capacity for success and its proclivity for failure.

As a utopian community, in contrast to an organization like an industrial firm, Oneida demanded complete commitment from its members. Unable to turn outward for substitute gratifications, they had to find all of their satisfactions within the Community. This total involvement heightened rather than reduced the possibility for conflict because Community leaders had ideally to satisfy the demands of each individual member's whole personality in the course of implementing Oneida's general objectives. Although Noyes had assured the Perfectionists that they would live in complete harmony and satisfaction within this framework, obviously it was impossible for the Community to be as good as his word. Many of Oneida's blessings were qualified ones at best. Members paid for group support with their privacy. For the sake of engaging in a range of sexual encounters forbidden in the outside world, they gave up the right to establish emotionally satisfying relationships, to experience the culmination of the sexual act, and to select partners of their own choosing. A member might have felt considerable satisfaction at his sense of earthly perfection or his expectation of finding happiness, but he was not protected from criticism when his outward behavior failed to reflect his inner perfection. For the right of participation in Community entertainments, members gave up the right to refrain from participation. Finally, it is doubtful that all of the people all of the time welcomed the Community's emphasis on educational endeavors.

How were Community members able to accept a way of life which, while it gave some gratifications, seemed so often to sacrifice individual interests to the welfare of the Community? One can certainly speculate that only a select group of people possessed the psychologial make-up that made Oneida Perfectionism truly appealing.[27] Perhaps part of its attraction lay in its promise of freedom from sin, its offer to extricate the believers from the psychological discomforts of unresolved guilt originating in their pasts. It seems unlikely, however, that members were drawn to Perfectionism solely for reasons of conscience: other people who suffered the oppression of guilt did not want to join the Community. Rather, members were perhaps, in addition, in search of some ideal person who would love them completely and whom they could love without risking the failure of an exclusive romantic association or disillusionment at the frailties which all human beings possess. For the women, the distant Noyes and the Community that he symbolized represented the ideal mate. For the men, love for a series of Community women and for their composite in the form of the Community answered their needs. Whatever fresh guilt may have arisen from the fulfillment of a desire for more than one sexual partner, even if such fulfillment entailed the rejection of a spouse, could be sublimated by turning over responsibility to a superior being—John Humphrey Noyes—or could be assuaged by observance of the built-in Community constraints such as mutual criticism, self-confession, male continence, and the preclusion of protracted romantic associations. As long as the personalities of the members remained constant and the practice of ideals continued, the Perfectionists would remain loyal.

There were other reasons for loyalty as well. First, having accepted Noyes's claim that he was God's representative,

[27] Other utopias have not needed to cater to or enhance such unusual psychological dispositions as those which Oneida sustained. Any group, if it is to embrace ideals different from those of the outside society, however, must select members carefully, the degree of care proportionate to the extremeness of its ideals. Thus the Shakers, with their rule of celibacy, must have had uncommon personalities. In contrast, people who join the Israeli kibbutzim or the Bruderhof communities of today need not have such unusual personalities in order to find membership attractive.

members who renounced their belief would admit their own gullibility. Were they to deny Noyes, they must also deny Perfectionism and, with it, their whole way of life. For some people the acceptance of existing tensions would have been preferable to recantation. In addition, personal doubts were to some extent avoided by a member's insulation from the outside world. Each person's daily routine in concert with Community routine acted out and reinforced Perfectionist ideals. The longer a member stayed, the more difficult it was for him to envision alternative ways of life or to consider alternative religious systems.

Although the members of the Community chose Oneida and, indeed, were chosen by it, their willingness to live by its principles and practices was only partially responsible for Oneida's survival. Equally basic to the success of the experiment was the coordination of members' activities into those of a smoothly operating group. John Humphrey Noyes's choice and interpretation of the ideals of self-perfection and communalism were essential elements in the Community's success. In them he sought a solution to the fundamental question of the relationship between the individual and society. He and the Perfectionists believed that they could create a society in which the application of their ideals was beneficial to the member and the organization simultaneously. Absolute coincidence was not possible, however. Noyes provided the value system with further latitude by his interpretation of self-perfection: it was to include sacrifice for the Community, the reasoning being that he who is selfless in his love truly approaches perfection. By such philosophical nuances Noyes was able to divert attention from individual interests, the pursuit of which threatened the loyalty of the participants.[28] In cases of conflict he gen-

[28] Communities which make less extreme demands upon their members probably find social control less challenging. On the other hand, if they cannot select members who are psychologically adapted to their way of life, they have more reason to fear that participants will fail to practice ideals. Such is the case with groups like the Old Order Amish and the Dukhobors, whose young peo-

erally managed to effect some satisfactory compromise. Some of the compromises were arrived at simply through faith in Noyes: believing him to be God's representative and longing for his praise, the members listened attentively to his words, read his works, and tried to behave as he suggested. Other agreements were reached through lengthy discussions in terms of Perfectionist ideals. From them the Community member derived not only solutions to immediate problems but also a sense of control and an awareness of the applicability of the ideals of Oneida.

One important aspect of the balance between individual and Community interests in terms of the ideals was the system of complex marriage. As Lewis Coser has pointed out, this extreme representation of communalism was of major importance in preventing any internal division of loyalties.[29] Thus, as we have seen, Oneida systematically discouraged, condemned, and punished exclusive relationships. The practices of mutual criticism and confession of present and past failings similarly served the solidarity of the group in that they placed the Community at large, not specific individuals, in the role of confidant.

As the members were to discover later, the balance between individual and group interests was not only delicate but also necessary for survival. Noyes's sensitivity to this fact caused him to allow for the fullest possible individual development in order to offset the personal sacrifices upon which the Community depended. The converts to Perfectionism would soon have left Oneida if Noyes had lost his creative control or abandoned his flexibility after selecting viable ideals and suitable members. Instead, together, he and his followers learned how to build and operate utopia. Whatever aspect of that way of life a member considered, he found it consistent with his professed ideals. From the number of

ple receive severe punishment when they show signs of being "worldly."

[29] The ideas in this paragraph come from a paper by Lewis A. Coser, "Greedy Organizations," presented to the Massachusetts Sociological Society, March, 1967, pp. 7–26.

meals he ate a day to the number of times he had sexual relations, he found that the Community demonstrated what it had asserted in print: its "constitution and by-laws [were] principles wrought out and embodied in [its] customs and institutions." [30]

Further evidence of Noyes's concern that the balance be maintained lies in the fact that sacrifices were not always the responsibility of the individual members. Noyes was just as likely to ask that the structure of the organization be adapted to suit members' needs or to correct weaknesses originating in his own miscalculations. Doubtless, the malleability of the over-all structure did more to stimulate loyalty than could have been accomplished had Noyes relied upon a single blueprint for community action. Its greatest virtue was, of course, that the structure, like the members, could provide leverage without violating the all-important basic ideals.

The Community prospered, too, because the main principles upon which it was based—communalism and self-perfection—loosely defined as they were, could be adapted to allow for changes in organizational needs. Thus, for example, when financial losses from farming plunged the Perfectionists into debt, no rules prevented expansion into commerce and industry. If the application of ideals had been specified more precisely or if Noyes had been less prepared to accept change, the Community's economy would have failed and the experiment would have been disbanded many years before it was.

There is no question that the early success of Oneida was due in part to the dynamic and inspired leadership of John Humphrey Noyes. As we have seen, it is not difficult to establish at least a chronological connection between Noyes's gradual withdrawal and the decline of the system. To link his leadership indisputably with the success of utopia or his inability to lead with its failure is impossible,

[30] *Handbook of the Oneida Community, with a Sketch of its Founder and an Outline of its Constitution and Doctrines* (Wallingford, Conn.: Office of the *Circular,* 1867), p. 11.

however. The Oneida experience provides no basis for such a judgment because it included no successor with whom Noyes can be compared and because it was undergoing so many other changes in addition to its change in leadership.

It is, in any case, a vague and misleading oversimplification to assign to a leader full responsibility for the success or failure of a utopia. To say that a utopia prospers because its leader can inspire faith or that it fails because he cannot tells us nothing about the way the group is organized. A single individual simply cannot be held accountable; in fact, in some utopian experiments—the kibbutzim, for one—leadership responsibilities can be assumed by the entire community. The way a leader inspires faith, the actions he takes to establish and operate the community, and the content of his message are far more significant considerations. Although Noyes cannot be separated totally from his message or his methods, they, not he, were basic to Oneida's success. The key was not the presence of a leader but the practice of Perfectionism.

Finally, in assessing the reasons for Oneida's successful utopian endeavor, it is important to remember that it was essentially a religious community. Communities of this sort characteristically have had a greater potential for survival because they have found it easier, in acting out religious convictions, to place ideals above idiosyncratic personal interests. As long as its ideals remained central in the lives of the members, Oneida was able to prosper to the benefit of all. The Community's minor problems—a successor for Noyes, the integration of its young people, the introduction of virgins to Oneida's sexual practices—took on major, schism-making proportions only when the decline in religion undermined the value system sufficiently to diminish the importance of ideals and, hence, to destroy the balance which had existed between the individual member and the society. Unable to survive for its own sake, powerless to expect the individual to sacrifice himself for so empty a goal, Oneida terminated the utopian phase of its existence.

IV
The Oneida Community, Limited: Ideology

THE NEW COMPANY. The Oneida Perfectionists spent the last five months of 1880 planning their retreat from utopia. The commission assigned the responsibility of reviewing proposals for the conversion of communal property into individual property met almost daily. Two or three times a week it presented a summary of its deliberations for discussion at a general Community meeting. Anxious members listened to the reports closely, knowing that their futures depended upon the solutions that would eventually be adopted. Some who had brought considerable capital to Oneida feared that it would not be refunded. Others who had contributed little money wondered whether they would be repaid for their services. If not, how were they to live? Less objective considerations were also weighed. Members argued eloquently for the needs of the elderly, who were quite unused to coping with the outside world. They pointed also to the plight of the unmarried mothers and their children. "By jolly, they've got to take care of the women and children." [1] All members deliberated the possible solutions, constantly tortured by worries about how they would make their living "on the outside."

Eventually the deliberations ended with the formula-

[1] Pierrepont [B.] Noyes, *My Father's House: An Oneida Boyhood* (New York: Farrar & Rinehart, Inc., 1937), p. 182.

tion of a plan that was both practical and acceptable to a large majority. The "Plan of Division" represented a masterly solution to Oneida's predicament. The Community was to be transformed into a joint-stock company, with each of its members receiving an appropriate number of shares. Those who no longer wished to stay at Oneida could leave for the outside world; the others could live in the Mansion House, paying for their room and board at cost. Able-bodied members who continued to work in Oneida's industries would be paid for their services for the first time, but wages would be kept relatively low in order for as large a share of income as possible to be paid in the form of dividends to all ex-members.

The Community estimated its worth, including the good will of its businesses, at $600,000. This book value was divided into twenty-five-dollar shares. Capital was not distributed equally but in proportion to the member's original financial contribution and length of service. Each member received stock equal in value to one-half of the property that he had brought into the Community. Widows' and widowers' stock allotments were determined on the basis of one-third and two-thirds, respectively, of the property they and their spouses had contributed. Anyone who had reached the age of sixteen while living at Oneida received a bonus of $200 in stock, and all children were to receive similar bonuses when they reached sixteen. After these provisions had been met, the remaining stock was distributed to members over sixteen in proportion to the time they had spent at Oneida since they had reached that age.[2]

The stock was divided among 226 people. Fifteen minors between the ages of sixteen and twenty-one all received relatively small amounts, and the distribution of shares among 210 of the 211 adults was as follows:[3]

[2] Robert Allerton Parker, *A Yankee Saint: John Humphrey Noyes and the Oneida Community* (New York: G. P. Putnam's Sons, 1935), p. 288.
[3] *Ibid.*, p. 289.

Stock	*Number of Members*
$674 or less	1
$675–$999	11
$1,000–$1,999	49
$2,000–$3,499	84
$3,500–$4,999	60
$5,000 or more	5
Total	210

Because Sewell Newhouse continued to oppose the Plan of Division throughout the breakup, his shares (not included in the above table) were held for him by another member. Five years later, at the age of seventy-nine, he finally withdrew his objection that, as the inventor of Oneida's animal trap, he deserved a larger share, and accepted his assigned stock. In the place of their allotment, two elderly members chose a guarantee of life support, and one other member accepted a small cash settlement.[4]

Although the months preceding "joint-stock" were filled with anxieties and disagreements, the principles of fairness and communal harmony prevailed sufficiently for the reorganization to be effected in a thoroughly orderly fashion. The Noyes party continued to look for guidance from their former leader, sending representatives to visit him in Canada. He stayed at Strathroy, near London, Ontario, for nine months and then moved 120 miles west to Clifton, on the Canadian side of Niagara Falls. Although most of the loyalists at Oneida still believed that Noyes was directing their return to the secular world, he never tried to resume control but continued, as he said, to let others rule: "Others can tell better than I how the rickety government which henceforth managed affairs at O.C. was established. My clearest impression is that it was to be run in my name, but was devised and engineered chiefly by Myron [Kinsley], with the help of the parties at home, and without much help

[4] *Ibid.*, pp. 289–90.

from me, except as I was a necessary dummy. . . . Myron really ran the machine and did pretty much as he pleased." [5] Noyes's perspective was limited and inaccurate. Kinsley worked closely with the other men who had been central members of the Community and who represented the two disputing parties as well as with Theodore Noyes's tiny neutral party. Together they directed the dissolution of the Community with considerably more executive ability than Noyes attributed to them.

ADJUSTMENTS TO JOINT STOCK. The formal transfer of Community ownership to individual stockholders took place on January 1, 1881. It brought some sense of security to the people whose lives had for months been plagued with fears for the future, but it was a long time before the hostilities created by the breakup were fully quieted and the process of adjustment to their new life was reasonably complete.

There was still much bitterness between the rival factions, and even individual families were divided in their allegiance. Ex-members loyal to Noyes separated themselves not only from the Townerites but also from those who had deviated in any way in their commitment to the aging leader. They met together privately, held religious meetings, and, instead of patronizing the new restaurant managed by a member of the Towner faction, opened another which was restricted to the staunch loyalists. There they restored the old Community's plain appointments and simple fare, simultaneously belittling the rival restaurant's fashionable tables and chairs, its waiters, and its "extravagant" menu.

For their part, the Townerites realized that they were in a clear minority. There was little likelihood of winning over the less committed persons and of obtaining a majority. Three Townerites served on the first nine-member board of directors that had been created with general Community approval during the months preceding the breakup. Sitting on

[5] John Humphrey Noyes, "Niagara Journal," Stone Cottage, Clifton, Ontario, MS, January 8, [1881].

the board with them were four men loyal to Noyes and two self-styled neutralists, Theodore R. Noyes and Francis Wayland-Smith, whose sympathies lay with the Noyes party. Consequently, from the start, the Towner group was outvoted. A year later, after the first company election, the minority group's representation was reduced to two: Wayland-Smith lost his place, and the Noyes party received a clear majority by taking six of the nine directorships.

Accumulated antagonisms cut too deep for the old Community principle of harmony to reassert itself; obviously Towner had no serious hope of playing a meaningful role in the new community's life. Soon after the first election in January, 1882, he migrated west, accompanied by about twenty-five supporters and followed soon after by several more. These ex-members made no effort to re-establish a community or to preach Perfectionism but established homes in Santa Ana, a new settlement south of Los Angeles, where many of them prospered. Towner himself became a county court judge.

In the first few years following the breakup several other groups of ex-members left Oneida. A few young people departed independently; eight or ten elderly men and women joined John Humphrey Noyes on the Canadian side of the Niagara Falls; and fifteen or twenty men and women went to work in the spoon- and chain-manufacturing businesses that the new company had moved from Wallingford and Oneida to the American side of the Falls, where they could use local water power.[6] The majority of stockholders stayed on in their old home, however.

Those who lived in the Mansion House had never known or had forgotten the ways of the outside world and had to make many adjustments to the new life. At the breakup, each retained furniture or clothing in his or her possession up to a value of thirty dollars and received a

[6] Probably those who decided to transfer these businesses to Niagara took no account of John Humphrey Noyes's residence on the other side of the Falls and were motivated only by economic considerations.

cash payment of sixty dollars. Many used some of this money to buy other Community property that was being sold to the members. For some, the most tangible evidence of Bible communism's end was the auction in the big hall: chairs, cushions, hoes, rakes, sleds, skates—all of the items not needed for the businesses—were sold to the new stockholders. The redistribution was only one part of the necessary readjustment, however. Members had to learn to manage their own finances, estimating costs of room, board, and personal necessities, trips to visit relatives outside, vacations, and cash needed for savings.

In the midst of their uncertainties, many stockholders started the new era with a frugality recalling the early years of the old Community. At the same time they treated others' property with the utmost respect: their scruples, it is said, required them to return even borrowed pins. Many felt that the costs of meals in the common dining facilities (provided by the company) and the rentals charged for rooms were excessive, but they were failing to take into account such overhead expenses as the upkeep of public rooms, the cost of heating the Mansion, depreciation, and capital investment. Others considered it unfair that men holding more responsible jobs should earn more than those doing unskilled work: previously they had all lived in the same fashion.

Outside the Mansion House, the ex-members could no longer brush aside ridicule with claims of Oneida's superiority. Parents faced new accusations of immorality; children, left free to roam in the village, heard taunts of "illegitimate" and "bastard." The hired men, who had once been required to keep their distance socially, now observed, "You Community boys will never be able to make your own way in the world; you will always have to stick by the Big House." [7] (By common consent ex-members were still called and called themselves community people, and their new company was referred to as the community business.) Many ex-members could at least claim the respectability of marriage or widow-

[7] P. B. Noyes, *My Father's House,* p. 178.

hood since most of the adults had joined as married couples and thirty-seven marriages had been performed at the breakup, but there were sixteen women under forty, twelve with children, who remained single.

In daily life ex-members had to take more initiative than had been demanded in the old Community. They had to reconstruct their social lives; they had to decide for themselves whether to stay with the company or to take their chances on the outside; they had to apply for jobs instead of waiting to be appointed; they had to determine their own talents and potential and train themselves accordingly; they had to determine whether or not college educations would be in order for their children, who, according to the guarantees established by the Community at the time of the breakup, would be educated free of charge only to the age of sixteen.

Ex-members also had to re-evaluate their attitudes toward religion. A number of them, especially the older men and women, continued to be loyal to Noyes's teachings until their deaths. A man who had been a central member at the time of the breakup wrote in 1888, "The matter of religious belief is now left entirely to the conscience of each individual." "Many, especially of the older members, adhere to the religious doctrines of the founder." [8] A few of those loyal Perfectionists had, of course, left Oneida in 1881, to join Noyes in Canada.

Rather than return to the aftermath of the breakup and the scenes of the past, John Humphrey Noyes preferred to remain at Niagara. For this reason he rejected the Community's offer of a private home near Oneida or Wallingford and accepted in its stead Stone Cottage, which the Community had voted unanimously to buy for him. For Noyes and the elderly loyalists who had joined him at his new home in Clifton, Niagara Falls, life became a microcosm of the old Community, with but one change: the participants did not practice complex marriage. Otherwise, according to

[8] Letter from William A. Hinds to A[nita] N. McGee, June 20, 1888.

Pierrepont Burt Noyes, his father was able to recreate Oneida's atmosphere of mutual enthusiasm.[9]

> The presence of Father Noyes was the outstanding reality in all our lives. Just how that presence impinged on boys—bringing in coal, cleaning the cistern, working in the garden or adventuring in the world outside—is beyond me; but memory asserts that it did add an imponderable something which gave to both work and play a peculiar zest.
>
> Old members of the Community have said to me that those who got within the effective area of Father Noyes's personality were reluctant to lose him; that life seemed brighter and more worth while when he was about. . . .
>
> [One such person said that] Mr. Noyes had no doubts regarding life or himself. He plowed through difficulties, disappointments and dangers with an inextinguishable faith in an Edenic world plan and the ultimate triumph of righteousness. He was a source of light and power for all about him.[10]

In this reconstituted "family," Henry Seymour, famous for his horticulture at Oneida, continued to supply the family's wants and succeeded in growing strawberries larger than any he had produced before. James B. Herrick, who had at one time been an Episcopal clergyman in New York, provided intellectual stimulation and helped to guide the household. Three elderly women, including Noyes's wife, took up the housekeeping responsibilities. Several of Noyes's children joined these Perfectionists at intervals. Other loyalists who were working in the company's Niagara Falls businesses visited the Stone Cottage family, accompanied by their wives and children. Some of these younger men and women built a communal house near Stone Cottage and moved in with the intention of sharing all their material possessions. But aside from this idea their new communal objectives were vague, and lacking the stimulus of general objectives, their plan never got farther than the creation of common dining facilities.

Life in the Stone Cottage household revolved around

[9] P. B. Noyes, *My Father's House,* pp. 224–28, 267–98.
[10] *Ibid.,* p. 297.

John Humphrey Noyes. He spent most of his time in detached contemplation and in reading the Bible. He continued to enlarge theologically upon Paul's writings, producing ideas which he occasionally discussed with his intimate associates. Sometimes, when the group gathered around him after the evening meal, Noyes was inspired to give a brief home talk. After the aging Noyes departed, those left in the living room followed their old practice of endorsing his words.

Noyes was willing to give ex-members living at Oneida the benefit of his advice and criticism in spiritual matters. He sent messages of hope, suggested courses of action, and offered criticisms that had lost none of their salience and cogency. But he never returned to Oneida. Only after his death in 1886, at the age of seventy-four, was his body removed to his old home. Over the preceding six years, time had mitigated the bitterness of the breakup, and the company officials sent a telegram asking the Stone Cottage inmates to bring Noyes's remains to the Mansion House. His grave in the Community cemetery is marked by a simple headstone identical to those found over the surrounding old Community graves. After Noyes's death, most of the men and women who had been living with him returned to Oneida to live out their days in the peace and tranquility of their old home.

By no means all of those who clung to the old Community's beliefs followed Noyes to Niagara Falls. Perfectionism was a way of life as well as a theological system, after all, and although many continued to assert their belief, the old vitality of their conviction was lost.

Some members who were disillusioned with Perfectionism returned to orthodox Christianity. George Campbell, the company president from 1884 to 1889, invited outside revivalists to conduct services that included hymns, psalms, and fiery sermons, all of which Noyes had outlawed forty years before. Substitute religion rarely proved very effective, however, and orthodox Protestantism never gained a firm foothold in the reconstructed community. For the most part religious interest of any sort gradually faded among the ex-members and their descendants, to remain weak for years.

Spiritualism for a while gained a number of influential adherents, and it eventually played a significant role in Oneida's development. The small group of spiritualists active after the breakup had been attracted to the occult during the 1870's. One of their most effective mediums, Clara Wait, had been reproved for her leanings toward spiritualism during her probationary correspondence with Oneida. Later Noyes himself had encouraged her and others' belief by admitting that, after all, spiritualism was consistent with his lifelong teaching about the possibility of communication with members of the primitive church. But he would never have condoned the developments that followed.

By 1883 a group of about six people at Oneida was said to have been receiving frequent messages from the spirit world. At first the messages reassuringly reiterated Perfectionist principles, suggesting, for example, that recipients strengthen their faith in man's victory over death. Later they took the form of revelations, telling the believers, among other things, to look for a third resurrection at which Noyes would be "Christ's chosen one to bring heaven and earth together." [11] When several such communications were reported to him, Noyes was thoroughly skeptical. He noted that the group had been "instructed" to keep all messages secret for the time being and saw this as an effort by "Hadean" spirits to confirm members' faith in the spirits before others could disabuse them. Scrupulous care, he said, should be taken in determining the truth of messages received. In the case of his own inspirations, he added, he kept a "pigeon-hole for language messages of all kinds which I label, 'Doubtful paper.' " [12] This reproof, together with the information that the Stone Cottage family was not receiving such messages from the spirit world, disillusioned some

[11] Letter from T[heodore] L. Pitt at Oneida to J[ohn] H. Noyes, April 11, 1883.

[12] Letter from J[ohn] H. Noyes to H[enry] J. Seymour, March 14, 1883.

spiritualists at Oneida but others continued their séances and went on grafting their new beliefs to those of Perfectionism.

The spiritualists' activities would have been of little consequence to the company had not one of their number, John R. Lord, become president in 1889, almost three years after John Humphrey Noyes's death. When Lord relied upon supposed messages from Noyes's spirit as directives for company management, Oneida's affairs deteriorated sharply. The stockholders watched developments with increasing alarm, knowing that the business had already declined during George Campbell's presidency.

The members' interest in the company was safeguarded by limitations on the sale of stock. Those guiding the old Community's reorganization had feared panic selling that, like a run on a bank, could ruin the new company or at least allow outsiders to take control and cease operating the business in the ex-members' interests. To avert such contingencies, they had proposed, with the other members' agreement, that for the first three years after January 1, 1881, no one should sell stock to outsiders without the approval of at least two-thirds of the directors and without allowing other ex-members a sixty-day option to buy. No such safeguards could conceal a lack of faith in the company for long, however. Even in 1883, the board of directors had been alarmed at the number of requests to sell stock;[13] as Oneida moved uneasily into the 1890's, the rate increased. Discouraged by these conditions, many younger men and women left to try the attractions of the outside world. By the end of the 1880's less than half of the original population of three hundred adults and children remained at Oneida.[14]

Spiritualism was not the sole cause of Oneida's economic problems. The company was in the hands of a conservative,

[13] Holton V. Noyes, "History of the Oneida Community, Limited: 1880–1925," taken from the minutes of the board of directors, with annotations by the author, MS, 1930, p. 47.

[14] Hilda Herrick Noyes, comp., MS Collection, and letter from William A. Hinds to Anita N. McGee, June 20, 1888.

elderly management accustomed to mid-nineteenth-century business methods. By the last decade of the nineteenth century, American industry had expanded considerably. Although small businesses still predominated, some great industrial enterprises had already been established. To succeed, a firm had to take advantage of improved mechanical skills, newly developed production processes, and new distribution and promotional techniques. Enmeshed in outmoded practices, Oneida's management was unable to innovate as the changing times required.

Pierrepont Burt Noyes. The man who eventually solved Oneida's economic problems was one of John Humphrey Noyes's children born during the stirpiculture experiment. His mother, Harriet Maria Worden, had been brought to Oneida at the age of nine by her widowed father. Twenty years later her father seceded, but while his three daughters remained on good terms with him, they chose to stay at Oneida. In 1870, the same year her father left, Harriet gave birth to the fifth of Oneida's stirpicults, Pierrepont Burt Noyes. (All Community children were given their fathers' surnames.) He was the second of her three children—an unusually large number for a Community woman to have. If his mother had married at the breakup, she might then have followed some other women's example and given Pierrepont her husband's name. But Harriet Worden could not marry any of her children's fathers. John Humphrey Noyes's wife was still alive, as was the wife of the father of her oldest child, born before the stirpiculture experiment; and the identity of the father of her third and youngest child, a daughter, was not known.[15]

Pierrepont lived the usual life of a Community child, with strict discipline, regular schooling, healthful diet, plenty of exercise, and careful training in unselfishness and cooperation. He suffered through the uncertainties of the

[15] Like other accidentally conceived children, this child was given her mother's surname.

breakup and the difficulties of adjusting to the new ethics and new ways of the outside world. Although he saw little of his father before the breakup, afterward he went twice to Stone Cottage, the second visit lasting a year.

Pierrepont became ambitious for worldly success early in his childhood, and when he was fifteen, he announced an urgent desire to go to college. His "uncle" Abram Burt, the father of Harriet Worden's oldest child, helped to scrape together the money needed for a preparatory year at nearby Colgate Academy. The following year Pierrepont was able to continue his schooling at Oneida because a number of the older men, impressed by the general wish among the children to go to college, had donated money to expand the Mansion House school into Kenwood Academy. Noyes graduated from the academy and completed two years at Colgate University. He then decided to return home and study for a scholarship to Harvard, but his efforts were cut short when his mother became seriously ill. When she died in 1891, Noyes, who had then been away from college for a year, gave up his plans for a formal education.

For a while he worked in the community industries, first at Oneida and then at Niagara Falls, but he chafed at the tight restrictions that the small, conservative company placed on an ambitious young man. In keeping with the old Community tradition, all responsible positions were held by the older, supposedly wiser, men. Like many of his generation at Oneida, Pierrepont saw little hope of advancement in the company, especially while he was a non-religious pragmatist and the president, Lord, was a spiritualist. With his half-brother Holton V. Noyes, another stirpicult, he left Oneida for New York City in 1892.

After trying a number of business ventures, the two young men had, by the end of 1893, established a sound and growing firm, Noyes Bros., Wholesalers of Silverware and Novelties. In it they benefited from their Oneida connections. Noyes's cousin George N. Miller, then working as the New York agent for the Oneida Community, Limited, offered to sell Oneida plated tableware and other products to them wholesale. He suggested that they act as jobbers and resell the goods to New York restaurateurs and owners of small stores. P. B. Noyes proved a persuasive, highly successful salesman, and the nascent company's business expanded. It profited further when the critical financial conditions of 1893 forced Miller to dismiss the wholesale salesman for his sales territory, which covered New England, Philadelphia, Baltimore, and Washington. Miller offered the job to Pierrepont on a split-commission basis, and Noyes took it, knowing that, as he traveled with expenses paid, he could sell for the Noyes Bros. company as well as the Oneida Community, Limited. There may have been some conflict of interests, but in general, he sold "Community" products to Oneida's wholesale jobbers and, acting as a jobber himself, sold Noyes Bros. products to some of the smaller stores in the same territory that he covered for Miller.

Early in 1894 Pierrepont and Holton dissolved their partnership amicably. Pierrepont kept the business, and Holton used his share of the capital to start a small restaurant in New York. Soon after, Pierrepont expanded his company further when James B. Herrick, after being dismissed from his position as Oneida's Chicago sales manager because of his strong anti-spiritualist sentiments, invested capital on an income-sharing basis.

Noyes's determination to be a worldly success did not cut him off from Oneida. Like many ex-members and descendants he kept in touch with friends and relatives from his old home. He, his cousin George, and his middle-aged half-brother Theodore, with both of whom he was then living, often visited Holton, who had recently married a young woman from Oneida. When, in 1894, Pierrepont married another of the stirpiculture children, Corinna Ackley, his New York household became a social center for at least six young descendants who lived nearby. (Reports of the couple's wedding, which took place in the Mansion House, illustrate that many ex-members and descendants had abandoned the simple ways of the old Community. The bride's trousseau was commended for its "completeness, elegance and taste," [16] and the surviving photographs of the large wedding party indicate that the members of the wedding were elaborately and fashionably dressed.)

At the time of his courtship of Corinna, who lived at Oneida, Noyes learned that the sixty-one-year-old Burt, one of the directors, was anxious to spend part of the winter in California and needed a substitute on the board of directors. Noyes, during his work for Miller and his conversations with friends at Oneida, had become concerned about the deterioration in the company's affairs. He and Burt talked together, and they agreed that Pierrepont should be suggested as his "uncle's" replacement. It must have struck the elderly directors as a radical proposal: Noyes, after all, was only twenty-three years old. Probably they argued that Burt's connections with Pierrepont justified his suggestion. Perhaps they also realized that Noyes understood the selling end of their businesses—and sales during the national economic crisis of 1893 had not been good. In addition, the position was temporary and on the powerless, minority side of the board. In any event, they agreed, and Pierrepont Noyes became a director in January, 1894.

Noyes's activities gave him an over-all view of what was going on in the company. He attended the monthly directors' meetings, and he acted as a regular agent for Oneida's products. His experiences convinced him that the company was being very poorly managed. He has documented how Oneida naïvely fell prey to unscrupulous profiteers and how it failed to adjust to the business world of the 1890's.[17] For example, some strong-willed businessmen had demanded and received special prices for their orders. This angered other wholesale customers who were charged the full price, and it also cut into Oneida's profits. At Niagara Falls Noyes found the silverware plant was manufacturing poor-quality goods. Surveying the whole picture, Noyes felt that, if mat-

[16] *Kenwood Kronicle,* I, no. 21, June 30, 1894, 1.

[17] Pierrepont B. Noyes, *A Goodly Heritage* (New York: Rinehart & Co., Inc., 1958), pp. 68ff.

ters worsened, the company might fail and the unsuspecting ex-members would be left without any source of support. He reported his concern to the friends in New York who had helped him with the Noyes Bros. company. Theodore Noyes, James Herrick, and George Miller agreed that Pierrepont should go to Oneida and instigate a proxy fight in an effort to break the power of the incumbent spiritualist party.

Noyes returned and led a fierce campaign. It was the sort of activity at which he excelled. A majority of stock was still held by Mansion House residents, but some of it was scattered far afield, held by ex-members, their children, and outsiders. Noyes visited many of them personally, urging them to vote their proxy for the anti-spiritualist party. The climax of the election was filled with such suspense that it was talked about for years. Nearly twenty-four thousand shares were voted, and Noyes's side won by a margin of only sixteen shares.

The new majority directors promptly offered Noyes the job of superintendent of the Niagara Falls plant, whose management he had criticized outspokenly during the previous two months. He accepted the job and soon proved to be the success that Abram Burt and his New York supporters had envisioned. Within a few years he rose through the company's ranks; shortly before he became thirty, he was in effective, if not formal, control of the Oneida Community, Limited.

A number of the older people at Oneida and some of Noyes's contemporaries later emphasized the self-sacrifice involved in Pierrepont's decision to give up his outside career and return to the home company. This, Noyes admitted, was only partly true. Oneida had, in fact, much to offer him. After he had led the successful proxy fight, he knew that company officials could not entirely brush aside his ideas, even though among spiritualists and anti-spiritualists alike there were people who regarded this new director as a brash youth. He also had a number of powerful allies in important positions, including some on the board itself. Consequently, he stood to play a major role in the direction of a small but promising business. If he could reach the top in management, he would, in effect, have a company of his own. There would be no outside directors and few outside stockholders to account to, and he shared common interests with the majority of stockholders—ex-members and descendants—in whose names he would be acting. Noyes's chances of success outside Oneida were, in contrast, promising but uncertain. His own New York firm was flourishing. With it he might eventually have earned far more wealth and prestige than he could have hoped for at Oneida, but the Noyes Bros. company was very young, whereas Oneida was an established institution with considerable capital investment and a solid reputation. Noyes, by returning home, did not so much sacrifice a great business career as gamble that his ambition would be better served at Oneida than elsewhere.

There was far more for Noyes to gain at Oneida than the opportunity to play a significant role in an established business with considerable growth potential. He had grown up there, and many of his friends and relatives remained. He was deeply attached to the Mansion House and to the friendships that it represented. In New York he had spent most of his spare time with other people from Oneida and had found himself involved with them in his business. Indeed, the city's lure of worldly wealth had been offset to some extent by the influence of such social philosophers as Theodore and George Noyes. They had encouraged his concern for the older ex-members who were dependent on the company for a livelihood and who were even less able to shift for themselves than they had been at the breakup fourteen years earlier.

Personal ambition, which Noyes considered so carefully when deciding to return to Oneida, was one of the outstanding features of his personality. What he described as a persistent "urge for success" [18] is seen in his adolescent goal of becoming a master carpenter; in his work at Colgate and his attempt to study at Harvard; in his move to New York, where business opportunities seemed far greater

[18] *Ibid.*, p. 210.

than at Oneida; and, finally, in all the energy and enthusiasm with which, after selling the Noyes Bros. company, he sought to build a new utopia in the reconstituted Oneida family. H. G. Wells, who visited Noyes at Oneida, described his attitude to business as "romantic." Business "had got hold of him, it possessed him like a passion." [19]

Fortunately for Oneida, Noyes's ambition was joined with a number of other characteristics vital for his successful leadership of the company. He was never discouraged by setbacks, considering them purely temporary: "he promptly forgot them and turned his attention to the future." [20] He loved any sort of struggle. A close relative says of him today that he never met any real unhappiness except for his mother's death. Perhaps this is an exaggeration, but certainly Noyes carried his personal enthusiasm through all his activities, whether planning a new sales campaign or playing golf in the winter snow with a red ball and a partner to help to watch where it landed.

In the business Noyes foresaw that traps could not continue to be Oneida's economic mainstay for long. He proposed that silverware should take their place. Many considered the long-established silverware market impenetrable, but Noyes was able to break into it by anticipating the significance of advertising in the American business world. In 1903, the year before he began his campaign, the company spent only $5,000 advertising its new high-quality silverplate. The next year Noyes out-argued the older board members and, using profits from the trap business, increased the advertising budget to $30,000.[21] From that time on, even during depressions, advertising remained a major item of expenditure. Before the demand for traps was seriously diminished, silverware had replaced them as Oneida's major industrial product.

The same enterprising spirit made Noyes take an over-

[19] H. G. Wells, *The Future in America: A Search After Realities* (New York: Harper and Bros., 1906), p. 164.
[20] H. V. Noyes, "History of the O.C.L.," p. 114.
[21] P. B. Noyes, *A Goodly Heritage*, pp. 194–95.

night train to Chicago after a misaddressed telegram informed him that another silverware company had failed to supply a hundred gross of butter knives and sugar spoons to be used for premiums by William Wrigley's growing chewing-gum business. Noyes's sudden appearance before Wrigley and his persuasive sales techniques brought Oneida the order, and a great many more such sales for many years.[22] On another occasion he assured a potential customer that a rival company's plated spoon had a steel base, not one of "white metal." When the spoon had been scratched to its metal base, he asserted that, set in water, it would become rusty by morning. He knew that it would rust, but he had little idea how long such a process would take. Fortunately his statement proved correct; he won the order and promised to ship the premium spoons at the rate of a hundred gross a day. This was another gamble: the factory had never before produced spoons at that rate, but Noyes calculated that it could, and it did.[23]

With people inside and outside Oneida, Noyes was a keen strategist, careful to retain their good will and to save their self-regard whenever they failed or were defeated. After winning the 1894 proxy fight and accepting the superintendency of the Niagara Falls plants, he kept on as many of the previous staff as possible. At Oneida the new majority directors agreed with him that members of the spiritualist party should keep their positions in management even when they had lost their places on the board. Thus, instead of flaring up, old antagonisms gradually abated, and Noyes eventually established a new organizational harmony at Oneida.

Noyes was well aware of his faults: realizing the dangers inherent in his excessive optimism and creativity, he relied on the devoted cooperation of his colleagues to offset them. As one of these men, now retired, put it, "He was a natural leader and, in spite of the fact that his enthusiasm sometimes led him into rather unconservative actions, he recognized that quality in himself and deliberately sur-

[22] *Ibid.*, pp. 144–46.
[23] *Ibid.*, pp. 135–36.

rounded himself with other men . . . who provided a sort of counterbalance to that—a financial conservatism that was necessary."[24] Noyes himself described the balance effected in a different way. He quoted a stockholder as saying, "I don't mind their turning control of the Company over to Pierrepont, as long as he has George and Stephen and Grosvenor hanging on to his coattails."[25]

Noyes's sociability was apparent in all his dealings with company employees, with men he met on his selling trips, and with ex-members and descendants of the old Community. Long the center of local social life, he gleefully tried his hand at every sport and every new enterprise. Treasure hunts, golf matches, cribbage tournaments, lectures, dances, experiments with extrasensory perception—everything attracted his curiosity and enthusiasm.

In later years some of the older men and women who still leaned toward Perfectionism suggested that providence had been watching over the old Community's affairs, preparing, through the stirpiculture experiment, the founder's successor. Certainly, P. B. Noyes was as anxious to lead as his father had been. By example and constant encouragement he urged descendants to devote themselves to Oneida, and as a salesman, manager, and negotiator he demonstrated shrewd, creative business skill. Soon family members at Oneida were convinced that he was leading them into a new era of greatness.

A New Idealism. P. B. Noyes's years in the Children's House and his adolescence spent among the ex-Perfectionists had instilled in him some of Oneida's old idealism and a sense of loss over the breakup of the utopia. Soon after his return from New York, he began to envision a new idealism

[24] As has been explained in the Introduction, I have not identified by footnote any of the people interviewed. Occasionally a respondent is identified in the text.

[25] P. B. Noyes, *A Goodly Heritage,* p. 148. The men Noyes referred to were his cousin George W. Noyes, Stephen R. Leonard, Sr., and Grosvenor N. Allen.

Whereas the porch over the main entrance of the Mansion House was built by the original Community, after the breakup porches and verandas were added to private apartments at members' own expense.

Photograph by Harry S. Jones

for Oneida, a new non-materialistic *raison d'être*. Social idealism remained a recurrent theme in his conversation. Men like Edward Bellamy and William Morris had responded to the problems of industrial society by creating new, imaginary societies in print. The last twenty years of the nineteenth century brought with them a spate of utopian plans and utopian novels—*Looking Backward, News From Nowhere, Erewhon*. Unlike those who explored the question at theoretical levels, P. B. Noyes, following his father's example, sought empirical solutions to the problems created by the developing industrial technology. Two sets of interests dominated his concern: those of the ex-members and descendants who worked in management, and those of the plant workers.

The idealism Noyes promoted in the plant involved the improvement of employees' working and living arrangements and their social relationships. He was later to implement these ideals by increasing wages, bettering conditions in the factory, instituting welfare and recreational benefits, and making Sherrill, the town in which they lived, an attractive and prosperous residential area.

Noyes proposed a very different set of ideals for the ex-members and descendants who worked in management and lived either in the Mansion or in the private houses that surrounded it. This new Oneida "family," separated from Sherrill in the area known as Kenwood, became the focus of his utopian idealism. As an individualist of Theodore Roosevelt's era, Noyes could not embrace his father's communalism. Instead he advocated for their small society what he called "a reasonable equality" of wealth, opportunity, and power.[26] A corollary of Noyes's ideal of near equality was his emphasis upon unpretentiousness, particularly upon unpretentious life styles. Another ideal was carried over from the old Community almost unchanged—the principle that a person ought to sacrifice his selfish aims to the interests of the group. The young man who typified the

[26] P. B. Noyes, "Basswood Philosophy, III," *Quadrangle,* II, no. 1, April, 1909, 10.

joint "society" of Kenwood and the company management must be intensely loyal to its ideals, ambitious for its welfare, ready with brotherly sympathy for every fellow member, and must have an honest, unselfish character.[27] Officials should work not for their own good but for the sake of organizational harmony. Noyes frequently urged them to develop the "amateur spirit"; like men playing amateur sports, they should work for the sake of the team's success, not their own. At all costs they must eschew the "professional spirit" which made men work largely for monetary reward, social power, or individual glory.

P. B. Noyes revived in part the old Community's ideal of self-perfection when he urged the ex-members and descendants to seek self-improvement. In a society of equals like that in Kenwood, he said, material possessions should not sustain faltering egos, and self-respect must come from the development of the inner self. All should have the opportunity to develop their talents within the firm and the Kenwood community.

Although Noyes believed that these ideals represented Kenwood's "community of aims"[28] and proved it was a new form of utopia, he could not establish a truly utopian community like his father's. John Humphrey Noyes had created the old Community according to predetermined ideals. In contrast, P. B. Noyes inherited an established social structure and had to work toward idealism within the limitations of this structure. The ideals he selected were already inherent in the Kenwood society or were easily accepted by men and women accustomed to Kenwood's way of life.

THE COMPANY MANAGEMENT. P. B. Noyes realized that the new Oneida, like the old, could promote no ideals unless it survived economically. In the old Community John Humphrey Noyes had contributed knowledge, ideas, and

[27] P. B. Noyes, "Basswood Philosophy, IV," *Quadrangle,* II, no. 2, May, 1909, 8.

[28] "The 1910 Banquet," *Quadrangle,* II, no. 11, February, 1910, 8.

general direction to the industries, but he never was vitally involved in them. In contrast, his son had a thorough command of all the new company's industrial enterprises, and the Oneida Community, Limited, owed its financial success to him. Obviously he could never have achieved this without the help of a loyal and talented management team; nonetheless, a frequent visitor to Oneida who was consulted on its business concerns correctly described the company in P. B. Noyes's day as "the lengthened shadow of one man."

When Noyes arrived at Niagara Falls early in 1895, to supervise the tableware plating and chain manufacturing plants, or "divisions," he first had to rectify the mismanagement that he had exposed during the proxy fight. For example, a small, private company which was buying large quantities of Oneida silver plate wholesale seemed to the older directors to be an excellent customer. Noyes saw that it was bad for Oneida's reputation and a serious loss of potential profits to have this company resell the silverware to the trade at retail prices undercutting Oneida's. Eventually he persuaded his board of directors to end this arrangement and to establish standard prices throughout the division's sales agencies.

In addition to such activities whereby he reorganized the management of the Niagara Falls divisions, Noyes worked hard at increasing their sales. His personal scouting expeditions soon brought the first of the special orders from manufacturers who, like Wrigley, wanted to use plated tableware as premiums. These occasional large orders supplementing the regular sales to small retailers did much to restore relative financial security to the Niagara Falls divisions and to contribute to the financial soundness of the whole company.

In 1897, the trap factory at Oneida, which had been the company's main source of income, was losing sales. Noyes's supporters on the board of directors suggested that he head this as well as the two Niagara divisions, but both company and old Community tradition dictated that the business departments should be left under separate control so that no one could monopolize them. Also, Pierrepont's youth still seemed a disadvantage to those accustomed to put their trust in the wisdom of age. As a compromise that would get Noyes's appointment approved, the elderly Theodore Noyes shrewdly suggested that the department should not be headed by one person but by a committee of three. The proposed composition of the committee, which included Theodore, made it quite apparent that Pierrepont would actually be in charge. The board acquiesced nonetheless, and the young Noyes left Niagara with his wife and baby daughter to return to the Mansion House.

Two years later, in 1899, the company announced its largest profits to date and paid its stockholders a dividend of 7 per cent. That year the board demonstrated its faith in Noyes by appointing him to the newly created post of general manager, with authority to oversee all the company's divisions—tableware, traps, chains, silk thread, and canning. There is no doubt that, in the years preceding and following this appointment, Noyes was largely responsible for Oneida's continued prosperity, but some part of the company's success must also be attributed to the general economic growth which marked the late 1890's.

The creation of the new post of general manager and the transfer of control to the young Noyes marked Oneida's emergence into the modern industrial world. At one time the business had relied primarily upon management's ingenuity, economy, and industry, and upon the excellent reputation of its products; Noyes introduced the new production methods, cut-throat competition, large-scale distribution methods, and all-out promotional efforts that were beginning to characterize American industry. He did not hesitate to use sharp business practices, some of which may even have been technically illegal but which were considered perfectly legitimate for an entrepreneur at the turn of the century. For example, Oneida joined with three other companies to fix prices of the "tie-out" chains used by southern farmers to pasture their cattle. A deal was made, but Noyes and the owner of one of the companies mistrusted the two other parties in the arrangement, believing that they would drop their prices below those agreed upon. Together they decided that when this happened they would reduce their own prices an additional 10 per cent. Evidence of their opponents' price cut soon appeared; immediately, Noyes and his ally made their agreed readjustment. They then set off on an intensive sales campaign, dividing the territory between them and eventually capturing most of the tie-out chain business for the year.[29] Time and again Noyes proved a hard man to deal with, but within the business ethics of the times he retained Oneida's reputation for integrity.

In Kenwood, Noyes's own reflections and his discussions with the ex-Perfectionists among his supporters brought into sharper focus his ideas about creating a semi-socialistic enterprise. This vision of a new Oneida with a modified communalism and a modified emphasis on self-perfection determined the direction of his search for the talented young men who were needed in the growing company. He began to urge descendants who had left and others who were still in school or college to consider a career at Oneida. Exercising all his persuasive powers, he pictured a rainbow that ended at home. The company, he said, had great potential as a business and as an idealistic enterprise. For the moment an elderly management was in control, but, he pointed out, he himself was already playing a significant role and, before many years, a number of retirements would open up positions in the firm's top echelons.

Young men did not find it hard to commit themselves to the welfare of an organization such as Noyes depicted. As one man from that generation said when interviewed, "There was an excellent opportunity here—not necessarily for making money but for development and for satisfying ambition. . . . I don't think those opportunities would have been so good elsewhere." Another man also referred to the opportunity for self-development in the business and

[29] P. B. Noyes, *A Goodly Heritage*, pp. 133–35.

to Noyes's belief that management should not be paid excessively high salaries:

> [P. B. Noyes] filled me with zeal. I came back with the strongest feeling of joining an active, aggressive organization. He gave us the contacts, meetings and discussions I like. He kept us all. He never tried to sell the material advantages of being here. He never did. No one who came here should expect to be rich. No one would lack, but never would they be rich. The idea of altruism is not hard to sell to the young. . . . It never would have occurred to me to come back if it hadn't been for P. B. I'd been indoctrinated with the idea it was a dying institution.

Men like these were not disappointed. At Oneida they found much to excite their interest and test their capacities. Louis Wayland-Smith, for example, found himself devising a detailed cost-accounting system that provided valuable quarterly reports for each department. He also set up a budgeting system and reorganized purchasing methods. Having headed the purchasing department for some years, he added the responsibility for the company's legal concerns to his work load.[30] In the early 1900's, before industry and government had become as complex as they are today, Wayland-Smith found that a one-year course in commercial law and a few years' experience in business outside Oneida were sufficient formal qualifications for him to prove eminently successful in his job.

Another descendant of the old Community, Berton L. Dunn, had trained as an eye, ear, and nose specialist and had been practicing nearby in Syracuse until he returned to Oneida in 1904. Noyes had just begun his silverware advertising campaign and had been borrowing the Quaker Oats Company's ideas of concentrating its advertising in magazines of large circulation, buying a whole page whenever possible. Instead of describing all its tableware at length, Oneida used most of its advertising space for a picture of one or two pieces of silver plate, which it often

[30] Louis Wayland-Smith, *Reminiscences* (Kenwood, N.Y.: By the author, 1955), especially pp. 8–9.

associated pictorially with someone or something attractive. Dunn took over this work. He began by showing Community Plate with handsome lace tablecloths and antique furniture. Later, in 1911 or 1912, he started a series of highly successful advertisements for which a popular artist, Coles Phillips, drew pretty girls holding Oneida silverware. Equally successful was his coup of a year or two later, when he persuaded such people as the dancer and arbiter of fashion, Irene Castle, to be pictured with dining tables laid with Community ware. These approaches did not really take hold in American advertising until the 1920's; thus, when Dunn started his work, he found plenty of scope for inventiveness in an area that today is a thoroughly specialized, highly competitive, and independent business.

Even men specializing in management could explore other areas. Noyes himself turned designer and produced Oneida's first "modern" spoon, "Avalon," on the theory that customers were tired of traditional patterns. He proved to be right. Another executive, aided by the artist Julia Bracken, designed the second of Oneida's modern patterns, "Flower de Luce," one that proved a Community Plate best seller for years.

The few men who had training in special fields also found ample opportunity to exercise their talents. Stephen R. Leonard, a mechanical engineer, constantly improved the production methods of the trap business and the quality and efficiency of the traps themselves. Later, when he had become a senior executive, he contributed many ideas to the department that had been founded in 1915 to coordinate and expand the company's welfare activities.

Many of the men whom Noyes attracted back to Oneida had been born there during the stirpiculture experiment or were the children of couples who married at the time of the breakup. By providing a school for the Mansion House children, the company had inadvertently created a highly cohesive group of young men and women who had attended classes together, organized dances in the big hall, produced plays, and taken "gang walks" in the snowy countryside, and who became deeply attached to the companions and the environs of their childhood. Even as late as 1935, twenty-four of the thirty-one stirpicults who had attended the Mansion House school were living at Oneida. Seven more who had left with their parents at the breakup had returned in the intervening period. All except fifteen of the forty-six surviving products of the eugenics experiment lived at Oneida or worked for the company in the mid-1930's.[31] Stirpicults or not, the young men and women who had been brought up together in the Mansion House eventually formed the core of the new Oneida Community, Limited.

Most of the men working in management had known each other all their lives and were friends as well as co-workers. Often they were relatives. Linked by strong emotional bonds to form the single Oneida family, they found that Noyes's ideals of teamwork and organizational harmony expressed their existing feelings about how members of that family should work together.

Noyes actually incorporated the principle of organizational harmony in an unofficial rule, adopted by the directors in 1905, that no important step was to be taken without consensus. The directors' decision was based on the assumption that differences of opinion could, in fact, be thrashed out or that some men would defer to the others' superior experience or competence. The assumption was false, but descendants' common interests and shared experience contributed to their willingness to accept the proposition.

In practice organizational consensus was not always easy to achieve, but Noyes's idealism provided a rationale for any minority to accept an unpopular decision. One diarist wrote, in 1915, about the election of two of the new directors: "No doubt there were heart-burnings and disappointments, but for the sake of harmony these were not voiced." [32] For herself, she interpreted the submission in

[31] H. H. Noyes, MS Collection.
[32] Diary of Jessie Kinsley (1914–18), January 20, 1915.

terms of their joint ideals: "I looked about and saw what I thought was a struggle with *self* marking some countenances."[33]

Management officials' concern for the company's interests at the expense of personal gain was encouraged by the nature of their financial share in the company. For those who held stock, what was good for the Oneida Community, Limited, was good for them, in the economic sense at least. Thus the proud older men had good reason for submitting to the demands of the youthful but obviously talented P. B. Noyes, who could justify his takeover as being in the interests of the whole group. As time went on, the older men could be persuaded to hand over their work to Noyes's contemporaries, who were better able to cope with the modern business world; but the younger men were prepared to leave apparent control in the hands of their seniors. The board of directors for many years acted almost as a rubber-stamp committee, discussing but rarely vetoing the plans of the small, informal executive committee led by Noyes. The board's minutes show that the directors talked at length about the degree to which the company should extend its businesses, the amount of money that was to be put into advertising, or the possibility of manufacturing condensed milk as a by-product of the community farm. The same minutes report the appointment of a committee to take care of the Mansion House lawns, an overpopulation of squirrels, and the dangers of children playing with matches in the Mansion House cellar.

Occasionally, Noyes found it necessary to deceive the conservative directors. Without their knowledge, in 1901 he directed part of the $30,000 appropriated for a new silk mill at Oneida into building facilities to manufacture the high-quality Community Plate which the company was to put on the market a few years later.[34] The directors' financial caution, however, forced the younger men to investigate a problem throughly and to back their position

[33] *Ibid.*

[34] P. B. Noyes, *A Goodly Heritage,* pp. 189–90.

solidly before they brought issues before the board. Clearly the directors lost control of the company, but the younger generation did not need, or want, to deprive their lifelong colleagues of their rank or their sense of contribution to a common enterprise. If they had tried, they would have seriously risked upsetting the general support accorded to the Noyes administration.

In the first years after Noyes took control, the younger men were not financially involved in the company to the same extent as their elders. They depended on it for their salaries but held little stock because most of them had received only small allotments at the breakup or had been given a mere $200 in cash on reaching the age of sixteen. But their financial involvement was soon to be as great as that of the older men. They agreed with Noyes that, although family members who shared their background and interests could be persuaded to approve of their plans for creating a new form of utopia in Kenwood, outsiders would not be interested. The way to secure themselves from outside interference was to buy back any stock which was now owned by people outside the family.

Management officials had little spare cash with which to purchase stock because, in accordance with company tradition, they received relatively low salaries. In 1898, Noyes began to urge the board to give these men, and himself, relatively rapid pay increases in order to finance their scheme to buy into the company. The board acquiesced and the younger officials set aside as much of their salaries as possible to purchase whatever shares came on the market. They even borrowed money, using that stock as collateral in order to purchase larger quantities. Breaking all the rules about diversification of investments, many took the proverbial risk of keeping all their eggs in one basket.

The attempt to "buy back the title" succeeded. Until well into the 1920's, family descendants at Oneida and elsewhere, along with a sprinkling of factory employees, held almost 90 per cent of the company's stock. For all the ex-members and descendants concerned, and especially for the new generation of executives, Oneida was not only their source of income; it was also the repository of their emotional social concern, of their utopian dreams, of their hopes for personal achievement, and of their material capital.

Although Oneida began to pay more to management, its salary rates remained lower than those of other firms. Noyes endorsed this practice because it implemented his ideas about Kenwood's being a relatively equalitarian community and because it showed that present officials, like those who took over at the breakup, were willing to sacrifice their own pay in order to give all family members dividends that were as high as possible. In fact, of course, dividends depended far less upon management salaries than upon production costs, total sales, and other factors. The significant effect of the low management salaries was the increased morale of the whole Kenwood community and of the plant workers; they believed that management was working for their benefit and not toward selfish ends.

In 1904, Noyes proposed another change that enhanced people's belief that management was working in the interests of the whole company. He proposed voluntary salary reductions for management whenever the company was in financial difficulties. The idea was accepted as a general policy, although no model for action was worked out. Profits remained so satisfactory that it was 1914 before the first such voluntary pay reduction took place. All salaried personnel then accepted a 10 per cent cut in their pay until the financial situation improved at the beginning of 1916. Later, in 1921, they responded to a more serious economic crisis by accepting larger cuts. Noyes halved his own salary, the directors took a one-third reduction, and the other officials took smaller ones in proportion to their regular salaries. During the Depression they responded similarly.

A complex pattern of shared interests united Oneida's

management. To everyone the "O.C.L." was of such vital interest that they found it hard to avoid shoptalk. In 1911, after an intensive selling campaign that scattered agents and management personnel all over the country, someone commented, "While the boys at their meals tried to stop talking silk, it seemed to be impossible. Silk was the only subject that was of interest to us." [35] The men enjoyed their joint effort to get out and sell more thread; it gave them another common bond and memory. It was, they decided, a modern version of the old Community's "bees." This kind of sales effort also benefited the company by affording management a realistic picture of the limited future of the silk thread after man-made substitutes had been found. The industry was sold two years later. (The chain business was sold in 1912, and three years later the canning business was discontinued because it was unable to compete with large-scale modern production methods. After the trap business was sold in 1925, the company's economy was entirely dependent upon silverware manufacture.)

P. B. Noyes fostered integration among Oneida's management officials, the other Kenwood residents, and the company's salesmen by instituting, in 1899, the popular "agents' meetings." The agents for Community products were called in to talk over sales strategy, new product lines, and ideas and problems. Like miniature conventions, the meetings combined sales planning and promotion with spirited social diversions. Some of the salesmen were descendents; most had had lengthy service with the company. With their wives and children, they joined Kenwood people in a round of dances, parties, sports, and excursions. Before long the agents' meetings, held in January and June, became the social highlights of the Kenwood year. At first they lasted only a few days, but by 1926 Kenwood's local publication, the *Community Quadrangle,* boasted two

[35] "Our First Selling Bee," *Quadrangle,* IV, no. 1, May and June, 1911, 4.

full weeks of activities—"An Agents Meeting that *was* an Agents Meeting." [36] In 1938, the meetings were no less popular. Those held in January ended on the twenty-ninth of that month, when

> A large gang gathered at the Oneida Station . . . to see off the Westbound agents. Bill Earl said there were more people than had been there since the first train on the Central went through. Jimmie Townsend was the only one to suffer any calamities. First he barked his shins by tripping over Doc Northway's bag. Then, as an Eastbound train whizzed past, Jimmie's derby went along with it. And saddest of all Jim optimistically bet with Harley that the train would be on time and agreed to pay a certain amount for every minute that the train was late. The train was very late.[37]

Kenwood sheltered its inhabitants from the conflicts and divided loyalties that often perplex workers in industrial societies. What one did for the business, he did for his community, his family, and his friends. No one had to look upon recreation as pure escape from work; the two were inextricably bound together. Even retirement did not require the construction of an entirely new life, for one could continue to live in Kenwood and gradually cease active involvement in the company while still keeping an interested eye on its affairs.

THE PLANT. P. B. Noyes often spoke of his plans for a semi-socialistic community that would include the descendants in Kenwood, the plant employees, and their families. From the earliest years, he tried to institute certain idealistic principles in the factory, but these were never integrated with the ideals he specified for Kenwood—personal improvement, organizational and family harmony, team work, relative equality, and a concern for all members of the

[36] [Pierrepont B. Noyes?], "Indiscreet Letters from Upstate" *Community Quadrangle,* I, no. 1, April, 1926, 14.
[37] *Community Quadrangle,* 2d ser., February, 1938, 14.

Kenwood family. The plant had no such pre-existing ideology for its employees to share. Instead, Noyes and other management officials instituted a series of improvements on their behalf.

The original Perfectionists had set a precedent in establishing good relations with their outside employees by paying relatively high wages and by providing good working conditions, transportation for some workers, schooling for the young workers, and other such benefits. For the period, these labor practices had been particularly enlightened. P. B. Noyes intended to do the same, and more, in his own era.

Early in his career Noyes decided that good wages were essential to good morale. In 1902, he averted the unionization of the silverware division at Niagara Falls by reducing the work day from ten to nine hours while keeping wages at the same level as before.[38] The change, he said, justified itself sufficiently to be extended to the other Oneida factories soon after.[39] In 1903, the board's minutes read: "A statement was made that our wages have advanced thirty or forty per cent." [40] In 1918, Oneida's overtime rates were increased from 20 to 50 per cent of the regular wage.[41]

Wages were relatively high, but the employees' work week was as long as that in comparable firms. In 1909, five or six years after Oneida had adopted a fifty-four-hour week for most of its factories, 90 per cent of the employees in all United States silverware and plated industries worked between fifty and sixty hours a week, while 82 per cent of silk industry employees worked between forty-four and sixty hours a week.[42] Ten years later Oneida's directors voted for a forty-five-hour week, leaving unchanged the workers' total wages.[43]

[38] H. V. Noyes, "History of the O.C.L.," p. 181.
[39] P. B. Noyes, *A Goodly Heritage,* p. 163.
[40] *Ibid.*
[41] H. V. Noyes, "History of the O.C.L.," June 23, 1918.
[42] *Thirteenth Census of the United States, 1910,* vol. X: *Manufactures, 1909* (Washington: Government Printing Office, 1913), 156, 306, 307.
[43] H. V. Noyes, "History of the O.C.L.," July 24, 1919.

At the same time that he was introducing these changes in wage scales and work hours, Noyes was improving the living conditions of employees working in the Willow Place factory, about a mile from Kenwood. In 1900 most workers lived four or five miles away in the village of Oneida Castle or the town of Oneida, but a few rented houses from the company near the Willow Place factory, although management encouraged these tenants to buy their homes.[44] Several years later the company was offering to pay 10 per cent of the cost when an employee built his own house.

In 1905 the company laid out plans for the community that was to become Sherrill. It determined the location of streets (naming them after members of the old Community) and the size of lots (88 feet wide by 165 feet deep).[45] It then was able to develop Sherrill systematically, opening streets one by one and providing each lot with the necessary sewerage, water, and electricity. Over the years, the company devised new ways to help employees to buy tenant houses or build on land bought from Oneida. Simultaneously the bonus paid to those who built their own homes increased in proportion to the cost of living. By encouraging workers to build for themselves, Oneida released them from the serfdom of company tenancy and escaped the danger of creating a uniformly drab company town.

Noyes's plans for creating an ideal community in Sherrill were further stimulated in 1913, when the company moved its Niagara Falls silverware business to Oneida. Since the chain company based at Niagara had been sold a year before, only the silverware division had been detached from the home company. To promote greater efficiency, management wanted the industries concentrated in one area, and Oneida was the obvious place. Furthermore, the Niagara plant was out-of-date, and the space available at that site was too limited for the expansion that the

[44] *Ibid.*, p. 157.
[45] P. B. Noyes, *A Goodly Heritage*, p. 164.

The Willow Place trap shop, standing alone in the 1890's, eventually became the center of Oneida's industrial complex although it was separated from the administration building in Kenwood by the Sherrill community.

Pierrepont B. Noyes, A Goodly Heritage (*Rinehart & Co., Inc.*)

company envisioned, whereas it owned a great deal of land near Kenwood. A special train was chartered to take 350 employees the 200 miles from Niagara Falls to Sherrill. They spent two days looking over their potential home. In comparison with the dreary town at Niagara Falls, Sherrill's well-kept appearance and the rolling countryside surrounding it were appealing. Of course, employment possibilities and personal considerations, like the problems involved in uprooting their families, must have been the major considerations in the employees' decisions; nonetheless, management's action encouraged some to move who might not have done so otherwise and boosted the morale of all those who did decide to go to Sherrill. These included more than half the working force, among whom were almost all major management personnel.

After the move from Niagara the company contributed even more to the development of the Sherrill community. Long before, in 1906, a clubroom had been made available to the employees. Now an O.C.L. Athletic Association was established, to which the company contributed an amount equal to the annual dues received. The old cow barn was converted into an employee clubhouse. An experimental five-hole golf course was created and a baseball diamond laid out. In 1917, $1,500 was spent on improving the roads and landscaping the industrial area.[46] Although very few Kenwood people attended church, the company contributed money for building churches in Sherrill. Originally the school district was shared with two other communities. In 1906, after agreeing to buy the Oneida school building and offering $1,000 in cash to each of these two groups of taxpayers, the company was able to persuade them to vote for separation. The new Sherrill school district was small enough for the company to contribute substantially to the quality of its educational system. Sharing costs equally with local taxpayers, it helped build a new elementary school and a new high school. In addition, it attracted

[46] H. V. Noyes, "History of the O.C.L.," April 3, 1917.

a well-qualified teaching staff by offering high salaries and an opportunity to live in the Mansion House. The interests of Kenwood children, who had been deprived of a good school since the Kenwood Academy was closed in 1894, may have predominated in the minds of some company officials, but management's actions were also beneficial to the families of employees.

Other ties linked the workers' families with the company. The welfare department was established in 1915. This was an enlargement of the old Sick Benefit Association, which the employees had founded in 1901 and to which the company had again paid amounts equal to the workers' contributions. The new department oversaw "house bonus" schemes and contributions to churches, education, and recreation. It concerned itself with employee loans, fire protection, an emergency nursing service, public health, and garbage collection. In 1916 its budget amounted to over $37,000.[47] The company began a group life insurance scheme in 1920 and a pension plan in 1928. The pension plan was not so far ahead of its times as most of Oneida's employee benefits: three out of the five other major silverware manufacturers had had comparable plans in operation for ten or even twenty years.[48]

Other benefits were provided to men who, in 1917, volunteered for war service. When they had dependents and their government pay was less than what they had been earning, Oneida made up the difference. Those volunteers without dependents received an extra allowance only if their service pay was less than half the amount they had earned at Oneida. With this plan the company was reviving a practice it had begun during the Spanish-American War.

In January, 1917, a new wage supplement was introduced, the high-cost-of-living wage. All employees earning

[47] *Ibid.*, p. 337.

[48] Murray Web Latimer, *Industrial Pension Systems in the United States and Canada* (New York: Industrial Relations Counselors, Inc., 1932), II, 1014–15.

less than $2,000 were eligible. The bonus started at 16 per cent of these workers' existing pay and was adjusted up or down in proportion to variations in the price index published monthly in Bradstreet's *Journal of Trade, Finance, and Public Economy.*[49] During this inflationary period, the bonus proved particularly popular with the employees. Unfortunately, however, prices rose so rapidly that by 1920 the high-cost-of-living wage amounted to almost half of each employee's salary. Because of the company's insecure financial position, the extra wage was stabilized on a basis of 50 per cent added to the base salary.[50] A year later, the market panic of 1921 found Oneida in very difficult straits. Noyes spoke to the plant employees; he detailed the pay cuts that he and the rest of management had agreed to and asked them to accept a similar one-third reduction in pay. In return he promised that, once the company was on its feet again, a new profit-sharing plan would be devised. The workers accepted Noyes's proposal. They probably had no alternative; but the spirit of cooperation with which they accepted the situation (and, later, the pay cuts introduced during the Depression) has lasted in the minds of the older men and the folklore of the company ever since.

By 1922, the company once again had profits to distribute, and a plan for sharing them that had been tentatively explored by one of the older directors in 1900[51] was revised and put into effect. There was no formal agreement as to how this "contingent wage" should be determined, but

[49] The company used Bradstreet's "index of commodity prices" that was "based on the prices per pound of ninety-six articles" including varieties of "breadstuffs," livestock, provisions and groceries, coal and coke, and nine other major categories. A summation of these prices produced the final index that in August, 1917, stood at $11.4414. "Commodity Prices Still Ascend," *Bradstreet's: A Journal of Trade, Finance, and Public Economy,* XLV, no. 2041, August 11, 1917, 513–14; and *ibid.,* no. 2010, January 6, 1917, 1. Oneida employees' pay was to be adjusted 1 per cent up or down according to each twenty-cent variation in this index.

[50] H. V. Noyes, "History of the O.C.L.," p. 380.

[51] *Ibid.,* p. 156.

in general, half of the company's profits were distributed to the workers in the form of an annual bonus determined by an employee's length of service, with some smaller variation according to the base pay he received. Take-home pay was further supplemented by a weekly "service wage," also based upon length of service to Oneida. For those who had been with the company for over twenty years, this service wage could amount to as much as 12 per cent of their base pay.

P. B. Noyes and other members of management illustrated their wish to give the workers a new kind of ideal community in which to live when they tried to persuade New York State governor Charles Seymour Whitman to make Sherrill into a "commune" that, unlike a regular village, would be detached from the outside world's Republican and Democratic party politics. In recent years one of the older descendants has described how Whitman eventually ended the long discussion he had with Oneida's Theodore H. Skinner: "I'll be God-damned if I'll have a commune in the State of New York. I'll help you make it a city." Thus, in 1916, Sherrill, which even today has a population of only 3,000, became a city and, according to the laws of the time, was governed by an elected commission and an appointed city manager.

Noyes believed that Sherrill residents, whether they lived in a commune or a city, could become as committed to Oneida as were the management officials and their families in Kenwood. Consequently, for example, he believed that the plant workers would be as willing as management to accept wage cuts in times of financial difficulty. But the idealism Noyes specified for the plant and Sherrill was quite different from that he specified for management and Kenwood. The plant workers were passive recipients of management's benevolence, not active participants in a new form of industrial "society." Like many other pioneers of industrial reform, Noyes failed to realize that all the power actually lay with management. Workers had little or no say in wage scales, the rates set for the high-cost-of-living wage, or the scope of welfare programs. In Sherrill, when they rented or bought houses, they could only choose from among the company's available tenant houses or the specific house lots it was then selling for development. Building bonuses were entirely at Oneida's discretion, as was the subsidy paid to the local school. The company, not the workers, decided to transfer ownership of the long-established Oneida store to the independent Community Associated Clubs in 1920,[52] just as it took the initiative in discouraging its officials from participating in the commission that governed Sherrill. This last action did, certainly, leave the Sherrill residents free to control their own affairs.

Noyes believed that if the workers were given power in the form of a union, conflict between workers and management would increase as each side fought for its own interests. He and the other officials were particularly effective in providing informal channels of communication: every plant employee knew that he could take a problem to "Ab" Kinsley, other members of management, or the president, Noyes, and that it would be dealt with fairly. Satisfied as they undoubtedly were, however, the plant workers could not be so emotionally committed to Oneida as P. B. Noyes envisioned because they did not help to determine idealistic principles governing their lives and because they contributed little to the practical application of those principles.

KENWOOD. In P. B. Noyes's day Kenwood was the unofficial center of Oneida, the home of management officials, the home of other family members, and the place where company offices were located. Circled on one side by the golf course and on the other by Oneida Creek, it was geographically isolated. Outsiders had little reason to go there unless they were using the county road that passed the front of the Mansion House and bridged the Oneida Creek at its entrance and exit from the "little world between the bridges."

[52] *Ibid.*, p. 378.

The ex-members and their descendants continued to live in the Mansion House, where they consolidated its cubicle rooms into attractive suites so that each family could have a spacious apartment which, by custom, was called its home. Only the common dining room remained as a significant remnant of communal living. With the changes, however, the Mansion could no longer house as many persons as it had in the old Community days, and as the business grew and the Kenwood population expanded once more, extra accommodations were needed. In addition, some people, especially young couples with growing children, sought more privacy than could be found in the old house.

In the early 1900's the company began to lease some of the hundred or more acres of the home domain to ex-members and descendants who wished to build private houses. Mansion House families and others who had been living in Sherrill or nearby began to build in what had been the orchard, around the piece of land that was once the old Community's vineyard, and along the public road that ran through Kenwood. By 1913, when the Kenwood population was about two hundred, nineteen families had leased land from the company and built substantial houses at their own expense. Year by year their numbers increased until the descendants had created a distinctive community in a beautiful rural setting, dominated by the Mansion House.

Kenwood couples had returned completely to the marriage codes of society at large. No remnant of complex marriage persisted; weddings were treated with all the celebration and solemnity customarily accorded them elsewhere. A description of Kenwood in the 1920's says that "divorce and infidelity are practically unknown." [53] Couples had as many children as did people in the outside world, and in the 1920's "families of three, four, or five [were] general." [54]

[53] W. F. Robie, "The Oneida Community and its Doctrine," in *The Art of Love* (Ithaca, N.Y.: Rational Life Publishing Co., Inc., 1925), p. 208.
[54] *Ibid.*

There is no way of knowing whether, if they did practice birth control, ex-members practiced male continence; however, three older men have written about it. In 1895, one published a novel that protested women's child-bearing responsibilities and advocated Noyes's "solution." [55] That same year, Theodore Noyes wrote that several of his Oneida friends practiced male continence.[56] In 1911, another man left a note to be typed by his secretary. It was in reply to a Boston bookseller's request for a bill for a copy of *Male Continence*: "In reply to yours of the 2nd. . . . The pamphlet 'Male Continence' is not sold by the OCL. It is out of print. I am with the Co. and happened to see your letter and sent you the copy from my private library on my personal responsibility. I will give it you, hoping that its contents will be a blessing to you as it has to me." [57]

Although they belonged to monogamous families, Kenwood residents were linked by numerous blood connections that had originated in the old Community and that, strengthened by their very complexity, had converted the Oneida Community, Limited, into an extraordinary version of a family firm. In 1908, twenty-seven years after the limited company was formed, fifty-eight of the eighty-nine family names listed at the breakup were found among people living in Kenwood and those working for the company but living elsewhere.[58]

Of all the generations of descendants, that of the stirpiculture children was the most cohesive and the one on which the ideal of commitment to the community rested most easily. Born into utopia, they were led, wondering, by their parents in the orderly retreat to conventional society; maturing, they shared the experience of adjustment to the outside world; and finally, they united to lead the way to what they saw as a new utopia.

[55] George N. Miller, *After the Sex Struck, or Zugassent's Discovery* (Boston: Arena Publishing Co., 1895).
[56] Letter to Rose Wright Bryan, April 2, 1895.
[57] Draft of letter from J. B. Herrick to K. W. Barry, June 2, 1911.
[58] Edith Kinsley, "Name," *Quadrangle,* I, no. 4, July, 1908, 10–11; and H. H. Noyes, MS Collection.

It was inevitable that outsiders should be introduced into the Kenwood community as descendants married outsiders and as the company brought in outsiders to fill management posts. From the breakup in 1880 to the mid-1930's, however, outsiders had relatively little effect upon the community's social structure. Even in 1935, only 63 of the 167 adults in Kenwood were outsiders, and about half of these were married to Community descendants. At that time there were twenty marriages in which both husband and wife were descendants.[59] Many residents were pleased with these "Community" marriages, believing they drew their society closer. Some did find the idea "a little bit incestuous," but in only a few cases were blood connections particularly close. One marriage that did meet with some protest was between a stirpiculture son of John Humphrey Noyes and one of the founder's granddaughters. The groom's mother and the bride's mother and grandmother had no blood connection with each other or with the Noyes family.

Many descendants were ashamed of or ambivalent toward their connections with the old Community's system of complex marriage and its extreme religious beliefs, but they were also very conscious of their shared past. By interpreting Bible communism as a sincere but misguided consequence of religious fervor and by seizing upon the acceptable characteristics of the original Oneida, they were able to look upon this heritage with pride. They reminded themselves of the Perfectionists' earnest belief in their religion; they pointed to the early privation undergone out of devotion to these beliefs; and they told themselves that the Community had been successful insofar as it had survived for a remarkably long time and had ended its days in financial prosperity. Thus they agreed with P. B. Noyes when he said that the old Community was "a genuine Christian Society where the teachings of Jesus Christ were maintained as rules for daily living. . . . Its founders were devoted to the Christian doctrines of unselfishness and consecration, and these were enforced in every department

[59] H. H. Noyes, MS Collection.

of human activity with amazing fidelity and literalness. . . . Mr. Noyes set before his followers the loftiest ideals of human relations and these ideals were realized to a greater extent, I believe, than was ever accomplished elsewhere." [60]

P. B. Noyes made much of the descendants' sense of group identity and past heritage. To him Oneida was "an organization which for its purpose is second to none";[61] theirs was "a society different from any other in the world," [62] one in which all felt deeply committed to the family group. As he expressed it for them, they were "one hundred people or more so close to each other that the sorrows or joys of one are the sorrows and joys of all." [63] They had learned "the real recipe for happiness, which . . . consists in doing something for someone besides ourselves." [64]

The ex-members' and descendants' social lives revolved almost exclusively around Kenwood and the family. They joined in such informal activities as croquet games, group outings, after-dinner discussions around the Mansion House fire, candy pulls, and parlor games, as well as in formally organized events. In the late 1890's P. B. Noyes revitalized the Sunday evening meetings that persisted as a last relic of the old Community's daily meetings. Removing the remnants of religion, he turned the occasions into purely secular affairs that included lectures, discussions, music, or reports of news from absent family members, including the "California migrants," many of whom had long since reestablished friendly ties with Oneida. In 1911, a general celebration marked the anniversary of John Humphrey Noyes's birth. Filled with enthusiasm for the new Oneida, many younger members had little interest in reviving the

[60] P. B. Noyes, "II, Basswood Philosophy. An Appreciation of the O.C.L.," *Quadrangle,* I, no. 12, March, 1909, 11.

[61] "Good Times for the Oneida Community, Limited," *Quadrangle,* I, no. 1, April, 1908, 10–11.

[62] *Ibid.,* no. 7, October, 1908, 8.

[63] *Ibid.*

[64] "H. V. Noyes, Toastmaster," *Quadrangle,* VI, no. 1, January, 1913, 10.

past for its own sake, but Noyes's centennial was, in a sense, their own. For a while, like the members of the old Community, they also commemorated February 20. At such a celebration in 1910, families from the outlying houses joined the Mansion House residents at dinner. Afterward one of the older men explained the origin of "the Twentieth" and described how the day had been observed when he and the Community were young. The "informal, spontaneous discussion" [65] that followed illustrates the Kenwood residents' efforts to define the ideals that represented their unique association.

George brought out, that however much the O.C.L. differs from the O.C., one strong factor is the same—the principle of Agreement, or united action—amounting with us to a religious principle. Pierrepont went on from that point to show that back of our spirit of agreement is a spirit of service for the good of all, to which personal ambitions are subordinated, and which has been and is the vital principle of the O.C.L. Dr. Cragin and Mr. Hinds spoke on similar themes.[66]

They concluded, finally, with general agreement, that such a meeting served to draw them all closer together.

Kenwood's life was provided with considerable social and intellectual leaven by a number of very able men and women. Among these were seven people who, between 1895 and 1935, published a total of fourteen books. Six of these were about the old Community or some other form of utopian society; the others ranged from esoteric literary biography to popular novels. Local poets contributed to the private Kenwood periodicals, and occasionally their works reached the pages of the *Atlantic Monthly* or *The New Yorker.*

The members of this intellectual group enjoyed the challenges of their jobs and the responsibilities of Kenwood's social life (although several, especially among the women, would have moved to a culturally stimulating city

[65] "Kenwood Journal," *Quadrangle,* II, no. 12, March, 1910, 10.
[66] *Ibid.*

The old Mansion House library contains books collected primarily by the old Community members. New volumes added continually over the years are housed in an adjacent modern room.

Photograph by Harry S. Jones

if their immediate families had not urged them to stay). They organized classes in French, painting, and music; they arranged or gave lectures on the gold standard, temperance, European history, children's diet, or Indian Vedanta philosophy; they organized social events, musicales, plays, and dances. Husbands and wives who made business excursions to Europe, South America, or Australia returned with experiences to recount and new ideas to try out. P. B. Noyes introduced golf in 1900, just six years after the first United States Golf Association was organized. Noyes brought H. G. Wells to Kenwood; another family invited Booker T. Washington; and when a descendant who taught at the Art Students' League in New York went back for a vacation, he was persuaded to give painting lessons to interested Kenwood residents.

Stimulated by these activities and supported by the family, all Kenwood people were encouraged to experiment with hobbies, sports, and intellectual endeavors that they would not otherwise have tried. One person experimented with a new form of braided rug woven into elaborate pictorial designs. Others took up painting, wood carving, drawing, and botany. Standards were high, and even when achievements were found wanting, Kenwood people's social support and advocacy of the ideal of improvement encouraged descendants to reach higher levels of success than they might have elsewhere.

In recent years comparable middle- and upper-middle class communities have sprung up a few miles away from Kenwood. But during the first part of the century Kenwood's psychological exclusiveness was enhanced by its physical isolation from any large city. Five miles from the town of Oneida, with its population of 8,000, it was twenty and thirty miles, respectively, from the two nearest urban centers of any consequence—Utica and Syracuse. Locally, Kenwood residents, like the members of the old Community, ranked high on the social scale. No other group was socially, intellectually, or economically more prominent, and the outside world of New York and Boston was too far away for members of the group to question their superiority. Consequently, few things encouraged the growth of the competitiveness of city life that was represented by fashionable dress, elaborate dinner parties, and expensive household furniture. Residents prided themselves on their lack of social pretensions. The wife of one important official esteemed for her generosity of time and money was teased admiringly for clothing herself in castoffs collected for the local poor. Residents frowned upon a young outsider who married a descendant in the late 1920's because she used lipstick and wore pretty "worldly" dresses. For her part, the outsider found Kenwood women frowzy and, exercising the individualism that Kenwood admired, continued to dress in the way she preferred.

When Noyes advocated simplicity, he did not mean excessively plain living: waiters served meals in the Mansion House and residents dressed for dinner; apartments were well-furnished and the new houses in Kenwood were large and comfortable. Rather, he advocated the degree of simplicity that was already practiced by the descendants and ex-members. He did not emphasize this or any other ideal unless it was generally accepted in the Kenwood community. Consequently, when he returned to the company in 1895, he was able to speak of the importance of commitment to the Oneida family. But it was not until a few years later, when the business was doing well and the company was growing, that he began to emphasize for the interlocking groups—Kenwood society and the company management—the virtues of self-development while working together as a team in an atmosphere of organizational harmony.

Noyes was never entirely clear in his expression of the ideals which he felt represented Kenwood. The ideal of equality gave him the most difficulty. When he first spoke about it in the early 1900's, the younger generation was only beginning to compete for executive posts on an equal basis with the older men. In the following years, the less capable descendants of all ages settled into safe management posts or, occasionally, into factory jobs. Like almost all of the descendants working at Oneida, they lived in Kenwood, but some did not feel entirely at ease there and drifted away, perhaps to live in the town of Oneida or the village of Oneida Castle, perhaps to take jobs elsewhere.[67] This scarcely perceptible selection by the descendants themselves contributed to the community's relative stability as an elite population. Its male members, backed by their wives, were often ambitious for a successful business career, but they were willing to measure their success by their actual achievements for Oneida rather than by their formal rank or their salaries and willing to temper their ambition for the sake of their commitment to the interests of the Kenwood family. Although these conditions encouraged the equality that P. B. Noyes advocated for Kenwood, certain gifted and idealistic people, anxious to pursue the new Oneida experiment, rose to the top as the company grew. Inevitably they became the central figures in Kenwood life, and although more than half of them came from families that had made no significant impact on the old Community's affairs, they were still seen by some descendants as a continuation of the first Community's elite. Probably because there was not true equality in Kenwood, Noyes would refer vaguely—and honestly—to its "approximate" equality.

Noyes undoubtedly felt responsible for implementing the admirable ideology that represented Oneida. Like those close to him he tried to exemplify the ideals in his daily life. In Kenwood he promoted social and intellectual activities that represented a continued effort at improvement, greeting plays, dances, lectures, and picnics with the same enthusiasm with which he devised new sales techniques. "Of course you must come. We expect everyone.

[67] For example, in 1909 an anonymous contributor to the *Quadrangle* commented, "There are a large number of former Oneida Community members—fifty or more, I believe—living comparatively near by but seldom seen here." "1909 Reunion," *Quadrangle,* I, no. 12, March, 1909, 3. A personal survey made by a Kenwood resident in 1935 lists at least twenty-eight families living in the surrounding communities. By no means all of their menfolk worked for Oneida. H. H. Noyes, MS Collection.

How can we be a family if you are not there?" Everyone who remembers P. B. Noyes speaks of this enthusiasm devoted to Oneida. A contemporary describes his efforts to create organizational consensus: "He insisted on cooperative effort. He could control organizational jealousies. He was a very, very frank person who would thrash out every problem. There would be fierce disagreements; but he would convince you or change his own mind."

Personal example was not enough to insure success, however. Perhaps one of Noyes's greatest talents was his capacity to edge people toward any specific goal while making them think that they were, in fact, acting in their own interests. His son[68] says of his leadership of the company, "Father was very, very smooth at moving people to places in a way that didn't hurt them, but *gave* them something." Other people felt he was too smooth, too persuasive, as when he urged an unwilling performer to participate in a concert or asked an older couple to move up to the Mansion and to leave their Kenwood house vacant for a younger couple. Still others felt he was paternalistic, acting on behalf of Kenwood residents but not allowing lesser people any established means to protest a violation of principle. As in the plant, there were many informal channels through which to present one's view, but there was no *guarantee* that a person would be heard or that the group itself would be the final judge of the application of ideals. Those who believed that Noyes was paternalistic were partly right, but he would not have been such a popular and effective leader if he had not acted in accordance with and promoted the general ideology that the descendants and ex-members themselves espoused.

[68] Pierrepont Trowbridge Noyes, present president of the company.

V

Oneida Ltd.: The Decline of Ideology

CHANGED LEADERSHIP. When the old Community officially adopted the name of the Oneida Community, Limited, in January, 1881, its action symbolized the end of utopia. In 1935 the company changed its name to Oneida Ltd. Although the change was dictated by purely commercial considerations[1] and held none of the grave significance associated with the original breakup, it again symbolized a new era. By the 1930's, the ideological community of the Oneida Community, Limited, was changing: its inherent ideals were becoming progressively more difficult to identify, and the community itself was moving closer to the ways of the outside world. The changes were to continue through the Second World War to the present day. Witness to the gradual decline of ideology throughout the years was P. B. Noyes, who had an exceptionally long career in the company—from 1894 to 1950—when he resigned from the presidency at the age of eighty. Throughout most of this period he kept close track of company affairs, attended board meetings, served on the executive committee, sought out new business, and de-

[1] The firm wanted to distinguish its better quality "Community" ware from several less expensive lines such as Wm. A. Rogers, which they had bought up and were continuing to produce under the original trade names. Some retail dealers capitalized on Community silverplate's reputation by indicating that the company's less expensive flatware was also "Community." In order to preserve their best product's reputation, the company decided to change its name to Oncida Ltd.

vised new selling techniques. He represented Oneida's interests with the local banks, with national organizations, and with the Federal government, in all of which, over the years, his gradually accumulated contacts served the company well. At Kenwood, he continued to be a social leader until age eventually made him inactive.

Although Noyes did much for Oneida throughout all these years, his concern was most intense in the period between 1894 and 1917, when he was rebuilding the company and defining a new idealism. In 1917, he resigned from the general managership, declaring that his action demonstrated his belief that the company should always have the benefit of young blood and new enthusiasms. He probably was convinced of this, but doubtless he also was glad to be free from keeping up with the day-to-day affairs of the re-established company and anxious to investigate new challenges. When, three months after he resigned, the United States entered World War I, Noyes was free to leave at once for Washington to see how he could contribute his services. Shortly after his arrival he joined the Fuel Administration, and by the end of the war, he had become the first assistant to its chief officer. The job brought precisely the sort of challenge that Noyes enjoyed. It was new; it required skillful maneuvering, manipulating, and bargaining within and outside Federal bureaus; and it gave him the chance to show how a businessman's skills could be adapted to a government bureaucracy. It also brought him into contact with men like Bernard Baruch and Alec Legge, President of the International Harvester Company. Noyes's absorption in Oneida had not abated his early ambitions to be near centers of influence, and he wrote proudly of such associations.[2]

In 1919, he returned to his work as an Oneida executive and set out on one of the frequent semi-business trips that he was to make during the next thirty years. On the way to Italy, where he hoped to capture some of the whole-

[2] Pierrepont B. Noyes, *A Goodly Heritage* (New York: Rinehart & Co., Inc., 1958), pp. 232–34, 239–50, 257.

sale trade for tableware "blanks" that a leading silver-plater in Milan had formerly imported from Germany, he passed through Paris. There he visited Bernard Baruch, one of America's representatives to the Peace Conference, which was then in progress. Baruch persuaded Noyes to serve on the Commission, which was appointed to resolve the problems of the Rhineland, a small but strategic part of Germany. The Peace Conference had decided on long-term Allied occupation and eventual demilitarization of the region; the Rhineland Commission, composed of representatives from the United States, Britain, France, and Belgium, was to work out the details—a complex task because of the differing interests and policies of the several powers. To help Noyes in this venture into international politics, the American delegation suggested that he choose as his assistant Wallace Day, a man who had served on the previous ineffective Rhineland Committee and who, Noyes said, would have been appointed to the Commission if he had not been so young. Noyes openly acknowledged how valuable he found Day's experience and skill in both government affairs and the problems of the Rhineland.[3]

Work on the Rhineland Commission was the type of activity Noyes loved. All his social, combative, and intellectual skills were exercised in the fourteen months of negotiations. He was particularly proud of a letter he wrote to President Wilson that influenced American policy and helped to untangle a difficult stage of the negotiations.[4] Outside his work, Noyes joined his wife and elder daughter in the social entertainments of the diplomatic world of Coblenz. By June, 1920, the Commission had completed the major part of its work, the Allies (with the exception of the United States) had signed the peace treaty, and Noyes had left the Rhineland.

[3] *Ibid.*, pp. 240–41.
[4] *Ibid.*, pp. 245–49, and Pierrepont B. Noyes, *While Europe Waits for Peace: Describing the Progress of Economic and Political Demoralization in Europe during the Year of American Hesitation* (New York: Macmillan Co., 1921), pp. 43–47.

It was fortunate for Oneida that its president returned in 1921 in time to help the company through the financial crisis of that year. Noyes resumed the post of general manager and spent the next five years watching more closely over the company's affairs. In 1926, he resigned from the post for a second time, retaining as before the position of president. The general managership was assumed by Miles E. Robertson, his son-in-law, a highly talented and effective executive who had joined the company in 1913.

Noyes was able to turn more of his attention to the social concerns that had crystallized in his mind during his work for the Rhineland Commission. He had already demonstrated that his interests had shifted to matters of far greater scope than the creation of an exemplary community at Oneida when, in 1921, he published his first book, *While Europe Waits for Peace.*[5] In it he argued against the Allies' punitive policy embodied in the Treaty of Versailles, saying that the economic problems and the social reactions resulting from the Treaty's provisions would precipitate further warfare. He proposed new measures for securing peaceful international relations, advocating, in particular, international support for the League of Nations. He was dismayed that the United States had not joined the League and argued eloquently for a change in policy. The themes found in this book were repeated in articles and lectures by which he sought to change Americans' attitudes toward their European responsibilities.

Six years later, in 1927, soon after handing over the job of general manager to Robertson, he published his next book, *The Pallid Giant.*[6] This science-fiction novel, which might well have been written after World War II, restated his fears that competitive armament would eventually destroy mankind. In a setting closely resembling Europe at the time of Noyes's work on the Rhineland Commission, the novel's characters discover and translate an ancient

[5] *Ibid.*

[6] *The Pallid Giant: A Tale of Yesterday and Tomorrow* (New York: Fleming H. Revell Co., 1927).

book relating the history of a race that had previously inhabited the earth and had eventually destroyed itself. The last survivor completes the history of his race with the words

> Fear, the child of self-love, both unchanged since the days when men were savages, unchanged through all the centuries while intellect was building to the skies material power,—fear desolated a beautiful world; turned the joyous peopled garden into an awful void of brown and yellow desert and naked mountains.
>
> My father Ramil saw, when the intellect of man had given to his unbalanced will a Godlike power of life and death, that then a love of fellow-men,—Mar-da,—alone had power to chain the wolf of fear. Then—it was too late!
>
> I, Rao, son of Ramil, last of my kind to look on this unspeakably lonesome, man-made desert called "the world,"—am ready to die.[7]

The novel's characters ask, "Is our civilization parallelling the history we have heard? Will our national armaments and national fears keep on stimulating each other until someone invents a modern Klepton-Holorif?"[8]—the all-powerful weapon developed from the extinct race's "study of atomic energy,"[9] the accidental consequence of which was mankind's gradual extinction. Noyes's whole book is a forceful, eloquent plea for an end to war and a new approach to international relations. However, being primarily a man of action, he did little to develop these powerful ideas. Time proved the validity of his concerns, but he himself gradually lost commitment to what proved to be one of the most serious problems facing twentieth-century man.

Noyes resumed his activist role in 1930. New York State's legislature had decided to build a new spa at Saratoga, and he was asked, again at Baruch's suggestion, to serve on the six-man commission responsible for plan-

[7] *Ibid.*, pp. 295–96.
[8] *Ibid.*, p. 297.
[9] *Ibid.*, p. 197.

ning and instituting the project. The job brought with it a trip to inspect European spas and a commitment to many years of responsibility: he remained on the commission until 1950.

Although P. B. Noyes was still deeply involved at Oneida, all his extra-community activities brought about a significant change in the nature of his leadership at home. He ceded direct control of the company to Robertson in the 1930's. After that he traveled to see customers, he attended his office, and he headed the executive committee; but often absent from Kenwood [10] and no longer the central figure in company affairs, he paid far less attention to the ideals he had once promoted. He retained his idealistic expectations about Oneida, but they lacked the relative specificity of earlier years. In 1926, on introducing a new series of the Kenwood periodical, the *Quadrangle,* he commented:

> We have grown so large that there is no possibility of all knowing each other or knowing each other's ideals or of moving forward together developing those ideals except through some form of written association. Many of the group know the Community ideas,—many more sense them imperfectly but would be glad to join fully in the O. C. L. group ambitions.[11]

And, displaying his uncertainty about what these group ambitions were, he continued:

> I have no fear but that the new generation will develop in a practical way the principles of the past, and will develop them to a point not glimpsed by us of the older time. We must be always practical, but we want to move continually forward as all life moves forward. The Quadrangle should prove a medium through which youthful enthusiasm can register its youthful ideals and assist the O. C. L. to move forward to accomplishments for which no man can set limits.[12]

[10] Noyes was so often away on semi-business trips that, after 1931, his teen-age son Pierrepont T. Noyes lived with his older sister and his brother-in-law, Miles Robertson.

[11] Pierrepont B. Noyes, "Editorial," *Community Quadrangle,* I, no. 2, June, 1926, 6.

[12] *Ibid.*

If that series of the *Quadrangle* is characterized by its failure to define Oneida's ideals, the following series, initiated in 1938, is distinguished by its failure even to mention them. Noyes simply wrote of company management and the Kenwood society's being "a group a little nearer together in our feelings than other groups," the members of which would be interested in hearing "the small items of news that are entertaining to one's family but hardly impressive to anyone else." [13]

As far as the plant employees were concerned, Noyes continued to envision Oneida as an example for the whole country. Years before, in 1913, addressing the assembled Kenwood residents and agents, he had said,

> The O. C. L. has grown into a large institution. We have done some of this work on the inside of our organization, and now it is up to us to make it one of our serious aims to co-ordinate our own developement [*sic*] with this great movement toward the amelioration of the working class. We must not go on blindly thinking we are doing enough. We must recognize what is coming. We must reach out toward the future with self denials and sacrifices. We are in a position to lead the way, are growing to a size which will make this leadership count in the issue.[14]

At that date he not only advocated improvement in the plant; he also had specific ideas for carrying out these changes—and he instituted them.

In later years Noyes merely urged upon Oneida the same general objectives for the plant, without suggesting how they should be achieved. During the Second World War, he assured the employees at the annual meeting that they would triumph in the hard work demanded by the changeover from manufacturing silverware to filling government orders for special sorts of hardware to aid the military effort. "Even in the face of necessary sacrifices," they

[13] P. B. N[oyes], *Community Quadrangle,* 2d ser., January, 1938, unnumbered first page.

[14] "H. V. Noyes, Toastmaster," *Quadrangle,* VI, no. 1, January, 1913, 11.

would still find happiness.[15] "I have great confidence in the future—and our future." [16] He would not, he said, allow idealism to disappear completely, even under the necessity of war production. He spoke of "the preservation of the spirit which for 50 years has made the company prosperous and a desirable place to work." [17] When, in 1950, he formally handed over the presidency to Robertson, who had in fact been the company's chief executive for years, he spoke on the same theme that he had introduced in 1913—the betterment of the status of the working classes. He suggested that, of all influences, ideas have the greatest effect upon the lives of men and nations. As the Russian people were obsessed with Marxist ideas so, at Oneida, they must "be obsessed" and "offer the teeming millions of the world a plan more attractive than Marxism" that "has a spiritual side of life, too." They needed to go farther "into the socialist field, meaning the creation of a more even spread of well-being among all classes of our population." [18] This would, he admitted, require increased taxes and other sacrifices. The speech ended:

> I am going to leave you with this thought. It is just possible that we Oneidans are in the lead in a movement towards a better and more practical revision of our business and social system than is Marxism: one that will spread the benefits of mass production and free enterprise more widely over the world's populations.
>
> I for one believe that even our rugged individualists will find greater pleasure when the wealth they think they have created is shared liberally with others.[19]

Whether he was speaking to the plant workers, the Kenwood residents, the scattered "family," the company management, the whole firm, or the complete industrial and residential complex, Noyes's exhortations never lacked en-

[15] Hilda Herrick Noyes, comp., MS Collection.
[16] *Ibid.*
[17] *Ibid.*
[18] *Ibid.*
[19] *Ibid.*

thusiasm, but in later years they became less and less explicit.

In the years after Robertson took over the post of general manager, he gradually assumed responsibility for the details of running the business. By the time of the Depression many aspects of company affairs were in his hands. The present company president supports the view of a number of older men who knew the situation intimately in observing, "We wouldn't have survived the Depression had it not been for Mr. Robertson, because the banks closed down on us among other things, but he was tough enough to show them. The banks believed in his toughness. They knew he could do it. . . . And Mr. Robertson had it going so well that in '33 we made money—and nobody else [in the silverware industry] did. We came back fast." Over the years Robertson's executive responsibilities grew as the productivity of the 2,000 to 2,500 workers increased and as the Canadian and British subsidiary companies expanded. Robertson handled his work with consummate skill, running the company according to the centralized model he had established during the exigencies of the Depression years. Since the old trap industry had been sold in 1925, a year before he became general manager, Oneida was a single-industry firm which lent itself to centralization more readily than a more diversified company would have. Perhaps Robertson chose his executive role partly in response to situational demands, and perhaps he also realized that this was the type of leadership for which he was temperamentally suited. In achieving the very important goal of continued economic prosperity, however, Robertson neglected P. B. Noyes's older ideal of maintaining a team spirit among management personnel. The consequences for management were not immediately apparent because P. B. Noyes and his lieutenants could still act as a counterbalance. However, men began to feel, as one person said, that there was "not the same . . . freedom to suggest and offer new ideas that there had been in an earlier day."

Robertson's approach to Oneida's idealism is curiously

ambiguous. In some respects he gives the impression of having been solely concerned with running the business, but this is a partial view which underestimates the degree of idealism in his thinking. While he might, as he said, have gone to Oneida simply because the company offered an attractive job, he certainly adopted some of its philosophy as the years went on. When in his seventies, echoing some of P. B. Noyes's youthful sentiments, he admitted that, once, money and progress had been of major importance to him but that, later, he refused offers of better jobs because he liked Oneida and the people there. As he put it, "It seemed to me there was a job to be done here; and that was an attitude I didn't have in the first ten years after I came."

Within a role more circumscribed than that of P. B. Noyes, Robertson chose to emphasize one major ideal: the welfare of all the company employees in management and in the plant:

> Coming in from the outside, and being the kind of person I am, I think it . . . would have been unnatural if I had not thought of the community as a whole—thought of *all* the employees. . . .
>
> . . . .
>
> I believe in a family of people working together to make money for themselves and to make money for the family: to have a good living as they went; to have a happy time as they went; to live together and to enjoy each other's company and to lay aside money for the day when it might rain; to play no favorites, to have no sacred cows. Everybody to be on their own according to their ability and what they were willing to give to the community as a family. And by the community, I mean three thousand people, not three hundred.[20]

As far as the Kenwood community was concerned, Robertson never tried to replace P. B. Noyes as social leader, partly because work occupied most of his time and partly because his commitment was to the whole industrial com-

[20] Noyes himself had occasionally urged that the Kenwood "society" be extended to include all the plant employees, but he had not done so as consistently as did Robertson.

plex, not Kenwood. The *Community Quadrangle* chided him for failing to contribute to its pages, but without any effect. He joined others at golf and participated in weekend ski trips, and for years on Sunday afternoons he joined a group of card players in the Mansion House lounge. Beyond this, however, he maintained social distance.

In the years following the 1920's both Robertson and Noyes worked in different ways to create some form of ideal organization out of the whole Oneida industrial complex. But as far as Kenwood and the company management were concerned, neither man worked effectively to keep alive the ideals that had been central to the philosophy of the Oneida Community, Limited. Then, as it happened, other developments had set in motion a spiral of change that even the two leaders' most valiant efforts could have done little to prevent.

CHANGES IN THE COMPANY. Throughout this century Oneida has continued to offer a significant challenge to the aspiring executive, and many young descendants have felt that they, like their parents, could realize their career ambitions at Oneida. The traditional emphasis upon improvement and education, however, has encouraged many of the young men (and the women) to take up alternative careers in the professional and technical fields that have been expanding rapidly during the last few decades. Unlike a few of the older generation, they have not been subjected to parental pressure to stay "home," and no economic crisis like the Depression has prevented their getting the training needed for a career away from Oneida. Gradually, therefore, it has become progressively more difficult to fill management posts with family members, and an appreciable proportion of the Kenwood population has become composed of outsiders. In 1935, 100 of the 167 adults in Kenwood were descendants.[21] Thirty years later the proportion was reversed: in 1964 there were 56 adult descendants and 83 outsiders. At that time half of the outsiders were married to

[21] H. H. Noyes, MS Collection.

Each morning most of Oneida Ltd.'s office workers enter the company's administration building in Kenwood, a few hundred yards from the Mansion House.

Walter D. Edmonds, The First Hundred Years (*Oneida Ltd.*); *photograph by Samuel Chamberlain*

descendants, but of these couples many were older men and women, and the proportion of younger people who were neither of Community stock themselves nor married to descendants was increasing rapidly. In the 1960's only 14 of the 89 family names recorded on the list of old Community members present at the breakup remained among the Kenwood population.

The community emphasis upon self-development and education had instilled descendants with the middle-class ethic of achievement in a career. For this reason, those who have stayed to work for Oneida, like the outsiders who have joined them, consider it important to be successful in their jobs and to move up the corporate ladder. This attitude influenced the response of almost every one of the officials who was asked what conditions would make him want to leave Oneida. Very few were actually considering leaving, but only one or two were so loyal to Oneida that they dismissed the question. Most of those who were committed to staying said that slow promotion in the company would be the principal reason that they would look for another job.[22] Descendants and outsiders gave similar replies: "Oh, [I would leave the company] primarily if I didn't make enough progress or . . . I was not as successful as I felt I was capable of being." Or, as another man expressed it,

> No, I can't say I have thought about leaving very seriously. I guess we all have our moments when we feel a little bit fed up with the job—feel that we are not moving ahead fast enough, but I would say that, by and large, during the years, I've been fortunate in moving along in the company. I've not gotten what I might call stagnant on any job, where I felt I was stuck there. So for that reason I think I would say I have never seriously contemplated leaving the company.

[22] The generalizations in this paragraph are based upon interviews with a sample of one-third of the Kenwood men and five management officials who do not live in Kenwood. In the remainder of this chapter, other such generalizations are derived from interviews with Kenwood adults, informal conversations, and personal observation.

Despite their expressed ambitions, descendants and outsiders have, since the 1930's, felt that Oneida offered less challenge than other companies and other careers. When they see people leaving Kenwood to take up different occupations and to achieve (apparently) greater goals, they sometimes feel guilty about working for a company in which everyone says a job is at least somewhat more secure than a job elsewhere. Insiders, that is descendants, feel especially vulnerable in this connection. Indeed, at least three of the present descendants observed the conflict in others and tried to avoid it in themselves by working in another company for a while after graduation from college. They wanted the experience, and they also wanted to prove that they could handle a job away from home. More significantly, very few men look upon a career at Oneida as giving the same opportunity for self-development that their predecessors saw there in the first decades of this century. They still believe in the importance of personal improvement but no longer believe that this can best be achieved at Oneida.

Some people at Oneida have, over the years, suggested that descendants have had greater opportunities for advancement and greater security than have outsiders. This was certainly true in the early years of this century, when Oneida's management was composed almost entirely of Community people and when P. B. Noyes deliberately encouraged family members to return to or remain with the company. At that time top management's preference for employing descendants and men who had "married into the family" was no more than an expression of commitment to the community. But, since outsiders were first recruited in large numbers in the 1930's, they have played a significant role in company affairs. No outsider held a seat on the board of directors until the 1920's, but by 1930 one-third of the directors were outsiders. In the late 1960's, over two-thirds of the board members were outsiders, as were over half of the firm's officers and over half of the executive committee. Talented outsiders have not been seriously limited by their lack of family connections since the 1930's and 1940's.

A high official descended from the Community and much respected in Kenwood by insiders and outsiders alike met the issue forthrightly:

> I think that being descended from the Community family certainly hasn't hurt anyone who has been in that position. . . . I think that Community connections, living in Kenwood, where, after all, the management of the company has traditionally lived, and being able to mix socially and to know personally the management does give you an advantage so that when there are two individuals with, let's say, equal ability, the one whose social contacts bring him into touch with the management of the company would be perhaps thought of first when an opportunity, an opening, occurred. Undoubtedly the factor of being a member of the family has been an advantage rather than a disadvantage but to exactly what degree it would be difficult for me to say. Since I, myself, have been the last ten or twelve years or more on the executive committee, participating in these decisions myself, I know that it is simply given no weight at all in promoting people.

Yet Kenwood people are not completely convinced. Almost every outsider, whatever his age, seems to feel at a slight disadvantage in the firm. On the other hand, half the community men believe themselves to possess a slight advantage and often feel a little guilty about it.

In the company management, P. B. Noyes's ideal of approximate equality of opportunity has been retained and extended to outsiders, but his ideal of approximate equality of wealth has had to be abandoned. Before World War II each newcomer to management learned that he "would never be rich" at Oneida, but the non-monetary rewards associated with his job were sufficient supplementary compensation: he could be party to the efforts by virtue of which Oneida became firmly established in the silverware market; he could feel a sense of personal commitment to the home community because his professional colleagues were, after all, his relatives; he could, because of the cohesion of the company and the interplay between his professional and social activities, be judged as a known and total entity. Since the war, however, the potential for intangible remunerations of this sort has been sorely limited, through no fault of Oneida's management: the effort to put Oneida on the map industrially, so to speak, has indeed been made and rewarded; the sense of family has been lost as the company has had to open its doors to outsiders; the resulting loss of company cohesion and the segregation of company and community have led to a situation in which one is judged in terms of his professional status and salary rather than his person and performance. Unable to offer its officials enough good will to fill out a non-competitive salary and unable to withstand the reduction in its ranks if it did not pay competitive salaries, the company had to abandon a principle—approximate equality of wealth—to meet a much more basic need—the presence of personnel.

By the early 1960's all those officials with base earnings of less than $20,000 were being paid at a rate comparable with that of other firms, and since then, the top executives' salaries have been adjusted gradually until today they also are about equivalent to those of other firms. While these salary adjustments were being made by the company, many people in Kenwood continued to believe, in accordance with tradition, that Oneida's officials were paid low salaries. Then, in 1966, for the first time, the proxy statement reported top executives' salaries in order to satisfy the rules of the New York Stock Exchange, to which the company was to transfer its stock from the over-the-counter market in the following year.[23] Kenwood resounded with surprised exclamations as retired personnel and people working in lower levels of management realized that top management had abandoned tradition.

Although in the 1950's management was gradually accepting the wage scales of the outside world, it still clung to another of the old customs—that of accepting salary cuts

[23] The aggregate direct remuneration of the eight senior executives was between $32,000 and $40,000, with the exception of one vice president, who received almost $44,000, and the president, who received $65,000.

when financial conditions were poor. In 1957, the directors responded to a report of low company profits by reducing their own salaries by 10 per cent. In the past such action had been seen by lesser officials and plant workers as an indication of management's commitment to the interests of the whole company: P. B. Noyes used to announce such salary cuts to the assembled workers while also explaining the reasons for the company's current problems and its plans to resolve its difficulties. The 1957 cuts in directors' salaries were not explained in such detail, and, lacking information, some people interpreted the action as top management's confession of failure. Furthermore, they feared that the traditional pay cut would soon be applied to them. Instead of improving morale, the directors' self-sacrificing action backfired. In order to check the rumors about the firm's financial condition, to counter decreased faith in management, and to improve general confidence in the company, the directors' pay cuts were restored.

Oneida's financial difficulties were at their worst when, at the end of the financial year January 31, 1961, Miles Robertson (as chairman of the board) and P. B. Noyes's son, Pierrepont Trowbridge Noyes (as president), faced an annual report showing a deficit: the company was still readjusting to the recent loss of government orders that, during World War II and the Korean War, had been a major supplement to silverware sales and had caused their work force to fluctuate from about 2,500 in 1939 to a high point of 3,800 in 1949 to about 2,000 in 1960. In adapting to the new conditions, the company had to develop new silverware lines, to consider introducing new products, to reorganize production, and to devise new advertising and marketing techniques. Its efforts have proved successful: confidence in the company has been restored as the balance sheet has improved, as employee bonuses have been distributed again, as dividends have returned to normal, as stock bonuses have been issued, and as the work force has expanded to over 3,000 persons.

Yet the very changes that management introduced to

restore financial security have contributed to the further decline in officials' emotional involvement in the company and have widened the gap between company management and the Kenwood community. In 1961, the year after he became president, P. T. Noyes introduced an outside efficiency expert to help evaluate the company's over-all organization of work. While it was completely in line with Oneida Ltd.'s long-term practices to employ modern business methods, it was not traditional for an outsider to be brought into the company without everyone's knowing why he was there and what he was doing. Anxious employees thought that the expert's arrival heralded a new era of increasingly impersonal management and speculated about "how many heads would fall" in their departments after he had left. In fact, no drastic reorganization of jobs was needed to restore economic prosperity, and the employees' insecurity has abated. The incident did, however, make at least lower-level management officials feel excluded from any modern interpretation of the team spirit of old.

In all areas of activity, management has continued to adopt increasingly formal methods. Objective measures of efficiency have replaced a more informal system of controls. Today, management as well as plant supervisors fill out for each person in their departments standardized job-rating forms designed by an outside agency, stating such things as a man's "strengths," "weaknesses," and "training requirements." Salaries too are no longer decided by a hit-or-miss method but are determined on the basis of an eleven-page questionnaire which each official fills out annually, describing the responsibilities associated with his job: his regular duties, the types of supervision they require, the scope of his authority, and his decision-making jurisdiction.

Oneida's officials react in different ways to this increasingly formal system of controls. A few men are beginning to look upon working for Oneida Ltd. as simply a job, not an avocation. One said, "I was hired by Oneida Ltd. for one purpose, and that was to do a job." Others consider the changes a result of top management's failure to promote the old ideals and its unwillingness to "keep out the ways of the outside world." As one man put it,

> In the late 1920's there was a different philosophy. I think that, in the years that have gone on since then, there has been a change in the dignity of the business. It has become perhaps more nearly like modern businesses everywhere, for all I know. But the management I think suffered from the older generation to the newer generation. . . . I think the socialistic atmosphere, if you want to call it that, was a very fine thing.

Still others focus upon the growing impersonality: "Management had a very personal approach to personnel problems . . . and today [it has] an impersonal approach. . . . With the impersonal approach I think you have more of the following of practice rather than, 'We want to try something new because we think it's got something.' " An occasional person, especially among those in the lower echelons of management and among the few descendants working in the plant, attributes the changes to top management's selfishness. As one Kenwood man expressed it, "All the economies are practiced on the lower income groups. The higher ones, of course, they stay right where they are." A Kenwood woman expressed similar sentiments:

> [Once] the men who were running this company were not out for themselves. They pulled together as a team. They each contributed as much as they possibly could. They didn't much care (at least it wasn't apparent that they cared) what financial reward they got out of this thing but what reward they totally got out of it. They said, "Let's make this thing go."

As far as many people at Oneida can see, in today's business world the only way to make Oneida "go" is to follow the path taken by present management—to deal with complex organizational and marketing problems in a formal, bureaucratic fashion. When the management was composed of a cohesive group of men sharing many interests, including a vital concern for their home company, group approval and disapproval were effective controls. But decreased group cohesion has led to the introduction of more formal methods of control which in turn have contributed to an even greater decline in group cohesion; thus, a spiral of change toward greater formality has shaped company policy.

Some of the same local developments that have required Oneida's management to approach its organizational problems differently have caused it to re-evaluate its role with respect to stockholders. Since the 1930's Oneida stock has been scattered beyond the hands of people working in or connected with the company. The change began after the Depression, when many descendants who held large amounts of Oneida stock felt obliged to diversify their holdings, and it has continued to the present as company officials, Kenwood residents, and descendants living away from Oneida have grown detached from the company and become willing to sell Oneida stock for more profitable issues. No one among the descendants or the newcomers to management has made any significant effort to prevent the dispersion. Today about one-half of the stock is still owned by management, by plant employees, and by pensioners and their wives and children. Community descendants own perhaps one-third of the total. The directors, including outsiders and descendants, do not own impressive amounts.[24]

More and more, therefore, Oneida's management finds itself responsible to outside stockholders who expect the company to be run like any other American business. A minority of outside stockholders has actually tried to gain representation on the board of directors. At the stockholders' meeting of 1964, these outsiders nominated two of their

[24] In 1966, the number of directors was reduced from 23 to 21. Some of these men held shares in trust. With the exception of these shares, according to the Proxy Statement of 1966, the directors together held about 50,000 of the 1,100,000 common shares outstanding. Six men owned less than 1,000, seven men between 1,000 and 2,000, five men between 2,000 and 3,000, and three men between 6,000 and 10,000. No director held more than 250 shares of preferred stock.

own candidates for election, arguing, just as P. B. Noyes had feared they would, that the incumbent board was not able (and, by implication, not willing) to protect outside interests.[25] Almost everyone in Kenwood owns some company stock, and in the proxy fight, they represented a significant proportion of the total vote. Many arrived at the spring meeting in the big hall of the Mansion House fearing that 1964 might bring a partial repetition of the old Community's breakup in 1880. They heard the tally of votes with relief: except for the attacking minority, almost everyone had voted for the selection made by the incumbent board.[26]

A few recognized that the meeting was symbolic of the new Oneida. One of these was an elderly colleague of P. B. Noyes. He had returned to Oneida in 1901, when the management was composed entirely of ex-members and descendants. In the days of greatest idealism, he had contributed talent, time, devotion, and capital to Oneida; as a young man he had done much to encourage others to keep company stock in family hands. Although the minority group's proxy fight failed in 1964, he knew it must bring change in the company. For the first time management's proposed slate of directors included three men who neither worked for Oneida nor claimed descent from the old Community. This addition of non-Oneida personnel to the slate was management's formal recognition of its responsibility to several different groups of stockholders as well

[25] The minority added weight to its argument by attacking the management of Oneida's subsidiary factories located away from Sherrill. Local stockholders might be persuaded more easily by accusations about plants with which they had virtually no identification. These other properties include a wholly-owned British subsidiary operating in Northern Ireland; a Canadian subsidiary that was 98 per cent owned until 1967, when it became wholly-owned; and a Mexican plant in which Oneida has a 50 per cent interest.

[26] On that occasion holders of common stock voted almost 97 per cent of the common shares outstanding. Eighty-two per cent of these votes were in favor of the directors proposed by the incumbent management.

as to plant employees and company officials. These new directors possessed eminent qualifications enabling them to give sound advice in the interest of the company's development. The retired executive was fully aware of this, but he could not resist commenting sadly that he had been there when P. B. Noyes had turned the Oneida family into an idealistic corporate unity; this election formally signified its end.

Few people at Oneida today would say that the company has lost all the distinctive and idealistic elements of the past. Men at every level in management feel that, compared with other firms, Oneida's management is less divided by personal conflicts and is more friendly. The president, P. T. Noyes, says, "There isn't the tremendous scramble that means you walk right over everyone's back. . . . I think it's more earnest . . . than other companies. The group atmosphere . . . isn't backbiting and scratching and gouging and so forth, and therefore they [the management] push down their own feelings of jealousy and envy and hate."

In the plant Noyes and other officials have retained the tradition of fair and generous treatment of employees. Practically everyone agrees with the president when he says that "Oneida is interested in every one of its workers . . . and their problems." They say that "Oneida Ltd. believes in treating its workers as human beings." "It is considerate of its employees." It always makes sure that it "gives them a square deal." This is not merely talk: wages at Oneida are about the same or a little better than those in comparable firms, and since 1964, they have been supplemented by bonuses. Furthermore, the company sells land at low cost to workers who wish to build their own houses and gives those who build a cash bonus of $400; it makes recreational facilities available to employees; and it has a welfare department concerned with employees' economic, medical, and even social problems both on and off the job.

But this type of concern for the plant employees, genuine though it is, derives from a paternalistic system that

Oneida Ltd.'s Sherrill plant
still includes the Willow Place works,
originally constructed by
the old Community.

Pierrepont B. Noyes, A Goodly Heritage (*Rinehart & Co., Inc.*)

is becoming less acceptable to the American worker. At Oneida, an advisory board composed of employees represents the workers' interests, but the present generation of workers is more likely to demand the real power given by some form of union representation. In fact, union representation would do little more than provide workers with a sense of autonomy, for the company has already introduced most of the improvements that a union might be expected to demand and some that the unions in related industries have not anticipated. With or without a union, Oneida could improve pension plans and increase insurance, hospitalization, and maternity benefits, but these are only elaborations of the existing material benefits to be got by working in any good company. Neither Oneida's management nor the unions have yet found what changes beyond material improvements will increase the satisfaction of the modern industrial worker.

CHANGES IN KENWOOD. According to Kenwood legend, a couple on a trip outside the community presented such an air of quiet contentment and self-conviction that they were mistaken for missionaries. "No," someone explained. "It is not religion that gives them this; it is a place." What it is about the place, what quality the community exudes that has come to be understood and referred to as the "spirit of Kenwood," has become increasingly elusive as the years have passed. Present residents particularly are hard pressed to describe in any meaningful way the ineffable atmosphere of their community. Most agree that Kenwood is an informal, friendly place with relatively few of the fierce interpersonal conflicts found in the outside world. Further, they agree on the attributes of a typical Kenwood resident: he should have a generous concern for others; he should be dependable, sincere, and unostentatious; and he should have a genuine sense of values. But when residents discuss the spirit of Kenwood today, it is evident that they are not thinking of group harmony, equality, simplicity, commitment to the commu-

Since the early 1900's, private houses have been built on almost all of the conveniently available land in Kenwood.

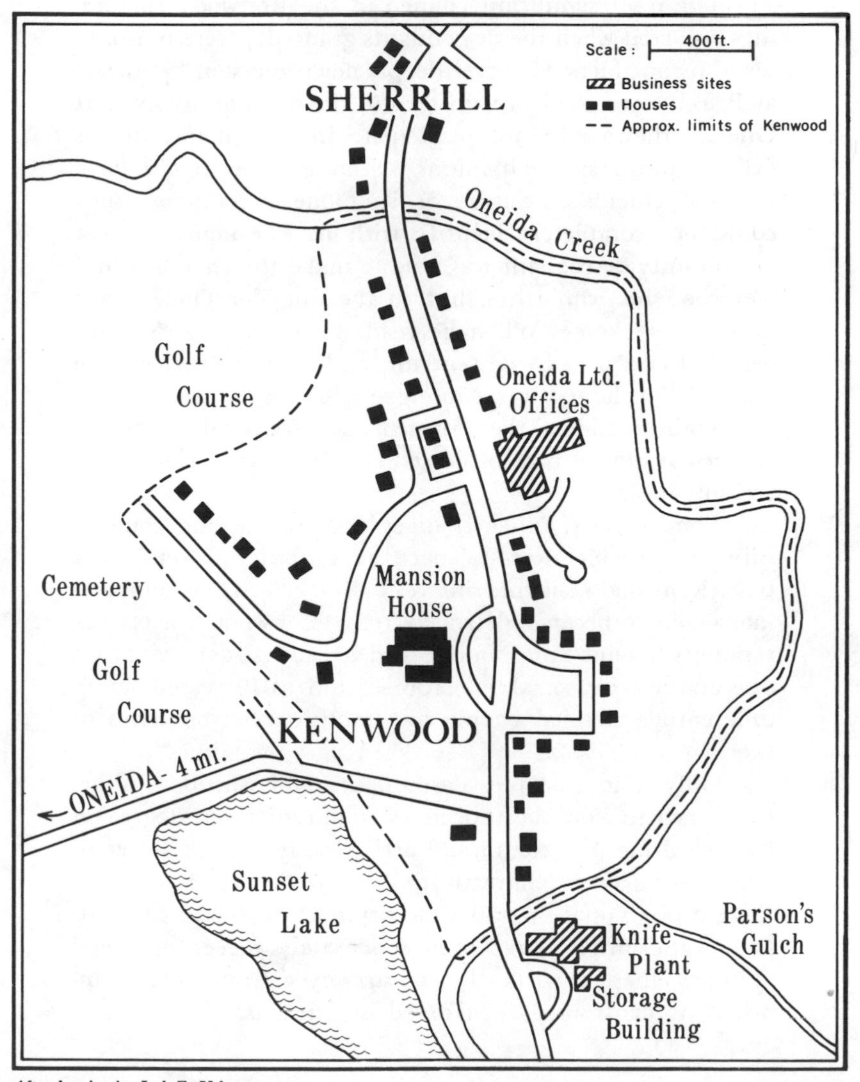

After drawing by Jack E. Usborne

nity, and self-improvement—the ideals that were a part of the value system fifty years ago. Without consciously contrasting the old and the new Kenwoods, most residents are nonetheless aware that their community is undergoing change: "Kenwood is becoming more and more like the outside world."

The most significant change in the Kenwood community occurred when the descendants gradually were outnumbered by outsiders. However deeply newcomers, or "joiners," as P. B. Noyes tried in vain to dub them, were involved at Oneida, they could not participate in the community as fully as did their companions. Although they might have admired Oneida's heritage or its modern company, they could not completely identify with it. For many years a Community descendant was able to make the company and Kenwood his whole life, but to the outsider Oneida was never really home. When he read the *Quadrangle*'s "Foreign Letters," sent by descendants and friends "abroad," he realized that he too was a foreigner. Because outsiders were to remain outsiders, they formed an increasingly large periphery around a core of descendants that was steadily decreasing in size.

Concurrently, other changes occurred at the community's center which were to affect the solidarity of Kenwood's base. Kenwood residents' interests diverged as the company management became detached from Kenwood society, as residents became more mobile and hence less dependent on one another for social intercourse, and as increased salary differentials enabled people to establish differing styles of life.

Only a few people, descendants and outsiders alike, have tried to slow the process of community disintegration by instituting new communal activities, fewer and fewer of which have been planned in the 1950's and 1960's. Although occasional events, a charity auction held at Christmas, for example, have been moderately successful single episodes, there is virtually no carry-over from one to another, no continuity of involved individuals.

In the absence of an all-encompassing social structure, the residents have reorganized into a series of overlapping but generally distinct cliques. Today a group of twenty-five or thirty people, including the president, exchange social engagements; several groups of younger people at lower levels in the management hierarchy share recreational activities and informal parties; and smaller groups of four or five persons enjoy common hobbies and interests. Twenty-five or so older persons are functionally isolated—no longer active in the firm, no longer a part of Kenwood life, and often without real friends: "I haven't got any. They're all dead."

The poignancy of the above speaker's words and the concise and straightforward presentation of the sense of loneliness so apparent in an interview with him in no way detracted from the air of dignity about him, a quality once advocated by Kenwood idealists, now ignored by those leaders whose energies by necessity are exerted instead in behalf of the company. The insular community atmosphere which at one time fostered self-improvement now seems not to enrich but rather to victimize some of those who have lived too long under its influence. As one outsider describes the process,

> This is a sheltered life, very definitely. You can look around and see some of them who have grown up here and never been out of the community, and you see they have come to have "Kenwooditis." I think this causes some people to have a lack of initiative, to become dependent on their community.

Insiders, too, recognize the "insidious lure" of Kenwood's security. According to one of them,

> Here, you have a large pool of comfortable people to be fond of. I think one great hazard, particularly for girls brought up in Kenwood, is the fact that their roots get too deep. They always feel like exiles anywhere else. They make sort of reluctant wives for people who have to live in a different area. . . . That is one of the great objections to a Kenwood bringing-up—to my mind. It just gets to seeming the only possible place to live.

Not all residents, of course, have succumbed to Kenwooditis, but it is the continuing emphasis on education that protects them, not self-improvement encouraged in its own right by leadership or buttressed as a positive value by group support. Most people do read widely, often judiciously, from the lists of current best sellers, documentaries, and histories; and many Kenwood living rooms are lined with shelves of carefully selected books. Many residents pursue hobbies like painting, photography, and the refinishing of antiques. Change has been felt even in this connection, however. Kenwood society once cushioned its members from the criticisms of the outside world and encouraged all, however untalented, to explore challenging ideas and activities. More recently, some residents have begun to ridicule the "tinkering" innovator and to disparage the amateur, discouraging the pursuits that once enlivened their daily existence and simultaneously gave Kenwood a part of its distinction.

Although Kenwood residents, through mobility, education, and the influx of outsiders, have become increasingly sophisticated and cosmopolitan, socially they are not excessively pretentious. Despite their income levels, most of them furnish their houses modestly, drive relatively inexpensive cars,[27] and entertain informally. As in the past, when it is economically feasible, they allow themselves modern comforts in the home and treat as a matter of course European vacations and week ends in New York City. Increasingly, however, simple tastes are giving way to more extravagant ones, as manifested in the amounts of money being spent for possessions and the growing emphasis on formal entertainment.

Most people living in Kenwood today, conscious of the impingement of new values upon their environment, have

[27] A list of all the cars owned by Kenwood people was ranked by two outside judges into eight prestige groups. I decided the few cases of conflict arbitrarily. The median car for all households fell in the fourth highest prestige category. I omitted from the analysis those couples with two cars.

The average Kenwood house is attractive and unpretentious.

Photograph by Harry S. Jones

demonstrated a desire to prevent further change, but the years when something might have been done are long passed. Ironically, when the opportunity was at hand, the residents in fact encouraged the communal disintegration that was at the heart of the breakdown of Oneida's ideology through their failure to incorporate outsiders into their society. While it is true that some of the isolation felt by outsiders resulted from their inevitable detachment from Oneida's past, much of it probably stemmed as well from descendants' discrimination against them. When asked about this matter, almost all outsiders who were over the age of forty and who had not married into the family either took a neutral position or said that they had felt somewhat left out of Kenwood life. The latter view is not without justification. A number of outsiders stated that it was more difficult for them than for descendants to acquire houses or apartments in Kenwood.[28] Occasionally they can point to descendants who work outside Oneida and yet have found homes in Kenwood. Even in death outsiders are excluded from the old Community cemetery unless they happen to be married to someone whose forebears lie buried in the grove of trees now surrounded by the company golf course: on "An island in / A golfing sea / Sleep those who supped / On strawberry tea." [29]

The membership of certain Kenwood organizations and committees similarly reflects the exclusiveness of insiders. The benevolent society is such an organization. Founded at the beginning of the century, this charitable trust was designed to aid needy descendants. In 1908, it offered membership to descendants of the original Community, and its bylaws allowed for outsider membership, subject to a two-

[28] Theoretically, at least, the company exercises veto power only in a sale. If, after an owner has arranged a sale, the company opposes the particular exchange, it can exercise its right to buy back the property at the agreed sale price. Indeed, these days, outsiders probably believe descendants receive more of an advantage from their family connection than they actually do.

[29] Dorothy Leonard, "Forefathers (Cemetery)," *Buttressed from Moonlight* (New York: Exposition Press, 1951), p. 52.

thirds vote of the society and payment of a small initiation fee.[30] The society's directors, almost all of whom have been insiders, have continued to operate the trust largely in the interests of family members or those who have "married in." At first, they were called upon to aid the elderly; today an occasional college student receives a small gift of several hundred dollars. Descendants have also dominated the historical committee (concerned with ordering and preserving materials relating to the old and new communities), the Mansion House committee (responsible for upkeep and maintenance of the Mansion), the lawn committee (responsible for the Mansion House grounds), and the library committee. As late as the early 1960's, the composition of these committees was strongly "family": only seven of the twenty-six people involved were outsiders, and only two of these outsiders were not married to Community descendants.

Most of these committees are today in the process of being inactivated or are, in effect, being taken over by the company management. The outsiders' under-representation on them therefore dramatizes a past rather than a present situation, one which the outsiders have accepted with remarkable tolerance: "I think there is a policy within the family, so to speak, that they will always look after the family first. And people know that. . . . Anyone would look after their own family first."

The lines of separation that have been drawn as a result of the exclusiveness of insiders and the segregation of outsiders become blurred with the passage of time and the increased numbers of outsiders. Only those people who have lived in Kenwood for a number of years are sensitive to and verbal about the distinctions that divided Kenwood. "As a kid," one woman said, thinking back to the 1920's, "I wouldn't have been an outsider for anything." Today's young people, outnumbered by outsiders and treated similarly, attach no special significance to their birthright.

Even to those who have been in a position to witness the

[30] W[illia]m A. Hinds, "The Kenwood Benevolent Society," *Quadrangle,* I, no. 3, June, 1908, 12.

decline of the spirit of Kenwood, the changes have been so subtle and gradual as to attract little notice, and only recently have people tried to explain them. Some residents see the younger people's lack of idealism as the cause. Others view the changes as necessary adjustments to the demands of the modern world. These explanations are as incomplete as the one heard most frequently: that outsiders have introduced new and alien styles of life. The newcomers have had a profound effect upon the old idealism, but they cannot be held personally responsible for the failure of the old way of life. Many of the outsiders, especially those who joined the community before the Second World War, became firmly committed to Oneida's idealism. If length of service is any measure of one's loyalty, outsiders have been as devoted as descendants. In the early 1960's, the median time both groups had spent with the company was twenty-two years—a long time to stay with any firm. Similarly, outsiders have been criticized for their pretentious new homes, but unlike the descendants living in Kenwood, they have not been in a position to inherit the older, less ostentatious housing and have found it necessary to build. Further, newcomers have made just as much effort to learn about Oneida's past as have descendants[31] and are as inclined as descendants to seek intellectual self-improvement through independent reading of a wide range of literature.

Whatever the opinion of insiders, newcomers to Kenwood have not imposed their worldly attitudes and values upon a resisting minority. Simply by their presence outsiders have weakened the bulwark of Kenwood's distinctive idealism—the persistent and powerful sense of community—for it was as communal involvement declined that Kenwood residents abandoned their search for representative ideals.

Caught up in the routine of day-to-day living, comforta-

[31] Of thirty-six persons asked what they had read about Oneida's history, nine descendants and ten outsiders had read between four and nine books about the old and new communities. (This includes a knowledge of the various series of the *Quadrangle*.) Six descendants and eleven outsiders had read fewer than four such works.

After the Second World War a new stretch of road was constructed behind the Mansion House, and six private houses were built facing the golf course.

Photograph by Harry S. Jones

ble and content in the serenity of their environment, Kenwood residents suffer no preoccupation with the changing community. For the most part they think about it only when urged to do so. Responses are as varied as respondents, but only an occasional person is as bitter as the one who said,

> The social changes go right along with the business changes. This business of them pushing everybody down to get to the top, no matter who they stamp on or who they hurt, has happened socially, too. "We don't invite anybody to our parties unless they are going to do us some good" type of thing. For me that is ridiculous. This isn't the way it used to be.
>
> . . . I can remember parties when everybody came. I remember dances when I was a child. Everybody was there. Everybody was friendly and happy, and everybody danced with everybody else. But it isn't like that anymore. The little groups who are cliquey go off . . . and drink together and who sees them on the dance floor or whoever dances with them?—nobody except their own little group.
>
> Heaven's sake! It is no more like the way the family used to be than. . . . This isn't more unique now than any other small town in the U.S. It used to be.

Although it has not moved quite so far toward the behavior and attitudes of the outside world as this person believes, Kenwood has changed markedly since the early part of the century. There is little to sustain residents' commitment to P. B. Noyes's original ideals, and Oneida's second period of idealism has all but drawn to a close. A few distinctive features remain in Kenwood as in the company management: geographical isolation still encourages simple living and still, to some extent, forces residents back upon each other; a few people continue to act in the old ways; and always there remains the prevailing but vague belief that there is still something different, something utopian, about Oneida.

Today the few people there who seriously consider in what form these utopian hopes can be realized echo a prevailing theme in contemporary American thought: utopia can and must be sought within the context of the existing society. They do not believe that a whole society or even a part of society can be made perfect, but they feel that Oneida is a particularly suitable place to begin social improvement. Pierrepont T. Noyes expresses their convictions when he says, "I believe heartily that the kingdom of heaven is on earth," and he earns their admiration for his attempts to find a cause from which to direct the founding of a new utopia.

KENWOOD TODAY. The lives of Kenwood residents today closely resemble those of people in other middle- and upper middle-class communities in the United States. Indeed, in many ways Kenwood is typical of prosperous suburban America. By such criteria as educational levels, occupations, interests, incomes, and personal associations, most residents rank not only above the neighboring Sherrill residents but above the average as well. High-level company officials receive salaries of over $30,000 a year; and while a number of residents earn less than $10,000, generally they are men who have just started out in the firm and expect their salaries to increase relatively rapidly.

The Mansion House continues to play a role in the lives of Kenwood residents. At retirement, many Kenwood couples, in deference to their age and in response to a certain social pressure to provide homes for young families, have sold their houses and moved to the Mansion. There they can enjoy the benefits of inexpensive room and board, light housekeeping responsibilities, and proximity to relatives remaining in the area. A number of women who have spent their married lives away from Kenwood but maintained their associations throughout the years return to the Mansion when their husbands die.[32] A new, unmarried employee may have a room in its "dormitory," and a young couple may start married life renting one of its thirty-five apartments. As their accommodation requirements change,

[32] Even if one takes into account the fact that men have a shorter life expectancy than women, male descendants who have worked outside the company are far less likely than women to return to Kenwood if they become widowed.

Generally, people living on modest salaries occupy this and other multiple-family houses, most of which are clustered near the knife plant.

Photograph by Harry S. Jones

couples customarily have looked for houses in Kenwood or have rented the company-owned apartments or duplexes in Kenwood's seven multiple-family homes. When the cost of housing is too high or when housing or rental space is unavailable, some couples move to Sherrill or to Kenwood Heights, the more scattered community on the other side of Kenwood.

Although for many years most Mansion House residents have been elderly, visitors and temporary residents have generally enlivened the atmosphere. A few selected teachers from the local school are still invited to board there. During World War II, a number of married women whose husbands were in the service lived in the Mansion with their young children. Today, outside businessmen, friends of Kenwood residents, and company salesmen occupy the various guest rooms, the latter conducting business at the Oneida Ltd. sales offices nearby.

Daily life in the Mansion House is presently far from "communal." Residents furnish their apartments according to their own tastes and financial capabilities. Most residents and Mansion House guests do assemble, however, for principal meals, which are served in modified, more-elegant-than-usual cafeteria style.[33] When the diners have collected their meals, they sit in the dining room according to a prearranged seating plan. A number of residents have added elementary cooking facilities and refrigerators to their apartments so that they can have some meals in private, but the space limitations in many apartments make the value of the facilities more nominal than actual: a good many refrigerators must be placed in residents' bathrooms, where they appear incongruous in view of the prevailing air of gentility.

Despite the familiarity produced by years of personal association, present occupants of the Mansion House treat each other in a rather reserved fashion—somewhat as if they were in a residential hotel. Gone indeed is the gay social life of P. B. Noyes's day. Instead of gathering for conversa-

[33] Occupants of the four apartments that have full kitchens only rarely take meals in the Mansion's dining room.

Mansion House residents decorate their apartments comfortably and tastefully.

Photograph by Harry S. Jones

tion after dinner, residents generally return to their apartments and their private activities, pausing only occasionally in the lounge or the library for a word about their families or, more rarely these days, about the company.

Although the old house dominates the Kenwood scene, it no longer dominates its social life. Very few "community" events take place there now, except for an occasional wedding of a young descendant or a funeral of an elderly descendant. Once, almost everyone went to the Mansion for Thanksgiving and Christmas dinners; now those who attend are chiefly those whose relatives live there. In contrast to the past, the separate activities in which the people of Kenwood engage vary with age, taste, and income, not with the participants' sense of utopian idealism or community. In the conduct of their activities, the people reveal the character of Kenwood: it is very much a community of discrete families.

In many ways the area has much to offer a family, particularly the children. With its physical attributes and its relative isolation, Kenwood is a haven for them. Aside from their capacity for endangering themselves, children need be wary only of the hazards of the public road which forms Kenwood's main axis, and it carries little traffic to concern them. They are therefore given considerable freedom and the choice of a wide range of activities. Parson's Gulch, a shallow, tree-lined tributary of Oneida Creek, and Sunset Lake, created when Oneida Creek was dammed to provide water power, offer enjoyment during warm weather.[34] The same is true of the great trees planted many years ago by the original Perfectionists and of the lawns of the Mansion House. During the winter the steeper slopes are used for sledding, and children can also skate on a small makeshift rink on the lawn. In any weather the Mansion House, with its intricate design and somewhat forbidding atmosphere, is a favorite haunt of Kenwood children and their companions, who often these days include children from Sherrill.

[34] Fear of water pollution, however, has discouraged some Kenwood residents from enjoying Sunset Lake, and its swimming facilities are used more by Sherrill than Kenwood children.

Like most of the Mansion House today,
the old children's wing to the left
of the main entrance is used
for apartments.

Photograph by Harry S. Jones

Kenwood parents, like many other suburban American couples, are concerned for the formal education of their children. Because the company no longer subsidizes the local school, the responsibility for providing children the best possible education falls directly on individual parents, as indeed it does elsewhere. Since most families in the community have two to four children, the financial burdens are apt to be considerable. Generally, Kenwood couples who can afford it send their children to preparatory schools for the final two years of high school in the expectation that they will be better prepared for college entrance examinations. Although not all children go to first-rate colleges, most boys and girls expect to do some college work before settling in jobs, frequently in professional fields.

In increasingly large numbers, their mothers are inclined to take on full- or part-time work when the children are in high school or college. A few do clerical work in the company offices, but in neither the present nor the past have women been elevated to responsible jobs at Oneida.[35] Rather, they tend to assume the kinds of positions that women have traditionally filled, as teachers, nurses, or librarians.

As other aspects of community and family life bear little or no resemblance to the old Oneida, so the sexual and marital patterns of contemporary Kenwood residents also are divorced from the ways of the past. If Kenwood differs from other communities in these matters, it does so particularly in its sensitivity to speculation about "what goes on at Kenwood." As might be expected, the company is equally sensitive to the possibility that the past might cast a shadow on the present. Although Oneida Ltd. uses its utopian past as a selling point and writes off the Mansion's losses as a contribution to public relations, it too avoids almost any reference to the old Community's marriage system. Perhaps it is

[35] The one noteworthy exception to this statement is Mrs. Harriet E. Joslyn, who used to be in charge of the silk mill. She sat on the board of directors from the middle 1890's through the first decade of this century.

overly cautious; at least, an episode related by a high company official so indicates: when a popular magazine printed a salacious article about John Humphrey Noyes and the original Oneida, management officials went to local stores to buy up all available copies of the issue.[36]

As in the period following the breakup, there is no evidence at all of any continuation of, or belief in, complex marriage in Kenwood today. Very few residents would be able either to describe the system accurately or to state the rationale for its original adoption. By the same token, only those with an intellectual interest in Oneida's history are aware of the past practice of male continence. Today the sexual practices and attitudes of Kenwood residents echo those of American society's most conservative elements. Not surprisingly, Kenwood's recent history includes a few cases of extramarital relations, and other instances have doubtless escaped public notice. Whether or not these render invalid the appraisal of the community volunteered by some of its residents—that Kenwood is more "moral" than comparable communities—it can be said with certainty that its sexual attitudes and practices are a far cry from those of the past.

The changes in the religious attitudes of the members of the community have been as profound as have the changes in sexual attitudes. After the breakup, in the late nineteenth and early twentieth centuries, the majority of the descendants had found a set of values and meaning for their lives beyond the framework of institutionalized religion but within the context of an essentially Christian philosophy.[37] Identification with the community was to Kenwood residents what identification with the church is to other Christians. The sincerity of their convictions lost nothing in its independence from orthodoxy. At the funeral of a young Kenwood woman, a resident spoke eloquently of her struggle to

[36] Donovan Fitzpatrick, "Father Noyes and his Fabulous Flock," *True; the Man's Magazine,* March, 1960, pp. 31–33, 68–69.
[37] For a discussion of the dimensions of religion, see Charles Y. Glock and Rodney Stark, *Religion and Society in Tension* (Chicago: Rand McNally & Co., 1965), pp. 18–38.

understand the seemingly meaningless suffering and untimely death of a beloved member of the "family":

In my suffering I was groping for relief. I prayed to be shown the meaning, and one night this truth took me by storm: that, if God should take only the old or the weak, the young and strong would feel secure in life; they would dare to put off the building of character, which is the purpose of life; they would dare to give all their strength and time to pleasure and business and selfish ends.

As we try to protect our children from mistakes to save them from suffering, so God tries to gently guide us; but when we will not learn, in His love He must force us to see the truth. I saw that God found in Jessie nobility of soul, youth, strength, all in a superlative degree, and He knew that the loss of Jessie would compel us all to realize that the kingdom of God is first.[38]

Throughout the years, as Kenwood has taken on more of the characteristics of the larger society, its religious philosophy has been channeled along more traditional lines. Descendants appear to have been somewhat more reluctant to follow than outsiders have, possibly because they have a history of a lack of concern for conventional, acceptable patterns of behavior. In religious attitudes as in no other aspect of modern Kenwood life, the descendant continues to distinguish himself from the outsider. Although some descendants have never become church members—perhaps their sense of community has continued to provide sufficient meaning for them—church attendance and membership have gone up as the cohesiveness of Kenwood has dissipated. About one-third of the present Kenwood population attends services fairly regularly, and approximately one-half are now church members. By comparison, almost one-half of all Americans attend church at least once a week, and two-thirds are church members.[39] Further examination of

[38] "The Funeral," words spoken by I[rene] C. N[oyes], *Quadrangle,* I, no. 7, October, 1908, 9.

[39] Benson Y. Landis, ed., *Yearbook of American Churches* (New York: National Council of Churches of Christ in the U.S.A., 1965), pp. 283, 280.

the figures for the people interviewed at Oneida indicate that descendants are somewhat less likely to attend church than are outsiders. An additional distinction between descendants and outsiders can also be made: a descendant is unlikely to be a church member if he does not attend fairly regularly; outsiders generally maintain membership even if they do not attend.

As far as present church affiliation is concerned, most Kenwood people, both descendants and outsiders, have remained, with the exception of four or five Roman Catholic families, within the major Protestant denominations. Two families belong to the Church of Christ, Scientist, and one belongs to the Society of Friends. Others of the approximately two hundred and fifty residents belong to the more common denominations, principally the Episcopal. Even in connection with its denominational affiliations, then, Kenwood has become a typical middle- to upper middle-class community.

Despite Oneida's history of concern for the rights of the worker and the one-time socialistic tenor of its official posture, politically Kenwood's basic position has not changed since 1909, when the *Quadrangle* proclaimed Oneida a "stanch" Republican center. The same issue reported that, acting in the company's name, someone had sent William Howard Taft a telegram on the occasion of his election to the Presidency of the United States, saying, "Please accept our heartiest congratulations. Business is already improving." [40]

Given the prevailing political attitudes, class status of the majority of the residents, and the comparative isolation of the community, one finds there a more liberal view toward social issues and more concern for the way others live than might be expected. Among the residents are found pacifists, fervent supporters of the United Nations, and members of civil rights and similar groups. One descendant has demonstrated her concern by joining one of the few successful types of utopias to be found today—a Bruderhof community. On

[40] "Kenwood Letters," *Quadrangle,* I, no. 9, December, 1908, 3.

the whole, however, Kenwood residents are not socially involved. Certainly one cannot imagine their acting as a community to make their opinions better heard. Only over matters such as the price of silver or import duties on stainless steel flatware does Oneida speak in a single tongue, but the voice is that of Oneida Ltd., not the Kenwood community.

John Humphrey Noyes's Perfectionism was an extreme interpretation of the nineteenth-century optimism regarding man's capacity for improving himself and society. At first, like most other idealists of the day, Noyes thought that his plans for effecting social change could be instituted within the confines of the existing society, but he eventually found that, as he interpreted them, Perfectionist principles implied a totally new way of life. Consequently, following the example of a minority of nineteenth-century social reformers, he founded a utopian community.

Whatever the nature of its principles, any community which, like Oneida, endeavors to put its ideals into practice throughout the whole of its members' lives has to establish and preserve a viable way of life within the context of a larger society operating according to alien ideals. Thus, the central problem for John Humphrey Noyes was to institute his religious teachings in ways that would maintain the Community as a distinct organization and simultaneously serve the members' needs. He dealt specifically with the potential conflict between the individual and the group when he selected self-perfection and communalism as the primary Perfectionist ideals, and he continued to do so when he organized Community life in accordance with these principles.

Although many disagreements could be resolved in terms of the common ideals, some conflict was unavoidable. Noyes settled such differences by emphasizing that part of self-perfection which included personal sacrifice to the Community. When disagreements were caused by the inevitable changes occurring within and beyond the Community, his belief in progressive perfection allowed him to reinterpret the ways in which his religion should be practiced and so adapt Oneida to new individual and organizational needs.

Despite the flexibility of the system, Noyes was unable to sustain utopia: even the most gifted and inspiring leader cannot continue, in the face of incessant internal and external change, to specify, implement, and reinterpret ideals and to select members—actions that would enable him to maintain the balance between individual and organizational interests. In every community which solves its initial problems, sooner or later attempts at adaptation result in violation of the ideals and the breakdown of members' united commitment to them.

Although one can, therefore, argue that no community practicing distinct ideals can be preserved, one need not deny the utopian dream that motivated the founders of Oneida and other communities—finding a better life. One may, however, deny that such communities ever realize their expectations: the practice of Perfectionist ideals and a belief in one's own perfection do not guarantee either happiness or the existence of an ideal society. In the case of the Oneida Community, in fact, it seems that the founders determined to make life better, but because of the excessive psychological demands made on the members, they succeeded only in making it worse.

Descendants of the original Community probably were happier in the new Oneida Community, Limited, than were their forebears in the original Community. Indeed, P. B. Noyes may well have achieved his objective of making them happier than people elsewhere. These personal satisfactions did not derive, however, from anyone's efforts to create a new utopian community founded upon principles which offered the rationale for its existence: Kenwood residents' satisfactions, like their ideals, depended primarily upon the "society" to which they belonged. That society, a unique product of a heritage reshaped by a new leader in a new age, defies re-creation.

If the present Oneida Ltd. is to continue its tradition of finding ways to improve people's lives, it cannot hope to do so by recapturing the past; neither can it be transformed into a new utopian community. As Oneida takes on more of the flavor of the larger society, it is highly unlikely—even inconceivable—that people there will share enough interests and be willing to sacrifice individual freedom to the degree required for the establishment and maintenance of a communal organization. There is every indication, in fact, that residents will pursue their present course away from identification with the community and seek instead individual identities and, so to speak, individual versions of perfection. In all probability not all individuals will reject Oneida, but those who choose it will do so because it is a personal utopia or, if nothing more, at least a place in which they want to live. As one member of Oneida's management views the modern trend, it is not, nor should it be, haphazard; it is a positive force to be employed consciously and with the full exercise of one's informed judgment:

> I personally am rather content with my lot in life but, like most fond and loving parents, I hope to see something better for my children. It is not readily available here—the opportunities are limited. I would like them to be more—I don't know exactly what to say—I would like them to be out and around in the world more. And then, in the event that after a certain amount of travel and education, they find this is a utopia, well then, all well and good, let them come back and make their life here. But they are going to be booted out of the nest first and then make their decision after that. Right now I do not want to see them hang around here.

Although some people at Oneida are sufficiently satisfied with their lives to consider the company utopian, management is not trying actively to create a modern utopia. Privately, many officials, encouraged by the generally altruistic atmosphere at Oneida, feel that the company can continue its tradition of finding new ways to make all employees happier. In fact, the structure of Oneida, like that of many modern corporations, is such that work can indeed be made more interesting and satisfying than was possible in earlier decades. Today, even at the lowest level in industry, a job can be made to offer more than monetary rewards. To do this a firm must make a deliberate effort to promote the self-responsibility and autonomy that enable an employee to contribute to the decisions affecting his life.[41] Although Oneida may move farther in this direction, it is unreasonable to expect that it can make everyone happy or eliminate all forms of conflict: obviously some people will contribute very little to the company; others will not want to exercise self-responsibility; still others will inevitably find work distasteful. The company can never expect to make workers' goals identical to those of the organization. Oneida cannot expect to be perfect. At most, it can seek to increase its employees' general level of satisfaction with their work.

Like most contemporary firms, Oneida already pursues some such idealistic objectives. By intensifying its activities it could adopt a new hope for the future, one appropriate to the subdued optimism of the twentieth century and more realistic than that of founding a perfect society, one involving only a part of society and a part of the workers' lives.

In the early years of this century, partly by accident and partly by design, P. B. Noyes created in management alone a kind of spirit of cooperation that proved to be advantageous to both the employees and the company. The contemporary need in industry at large and at Oneida Ltd. in particular is to repeat P. B. Noyes's achievements within the context of the whole firm by restructuring industry as John Humphrey Noyes once restructured society.

[41] For a fuller discussion of these ideas, see John Kenneth Galbraith, *The New Industrial State* (Boston: Houghton Mifflin Co., 1967); Bertrand de Jouvenel, "Utopia for Practical Purposes," *Daedalus,* Spring, 1965, pp. 437–53; Douglas McGregor, *The Human Side of Enterprise* (New York: McGraw-Hill Book Co., 1960); Mark van de Vall, *Labor Organization* (Cambridge: At the University Press, 1969), chap. II; and Paul Blumberg, *Industrial Democracy, the Sociology of Participation* (London: Constable and Co., Ltd., 1968).

Bibliography

This bibliography is limited to sources giving at least some significant firsthand information on Oneida and to relevant works published by members of the original Community and its successor. Only first editions are listed.

Books and Articles

Barron, Alfred, and Miller, George Noyes, eds. *Home-Talks by John Humphrey Noyes.* Vol. I. Oneida, N.Y.: Oneida Community, 1875. Only Volume I was published.

Carmer, Carl. "A Reporter at Large. Children of the Kingdom." *The New Yorker,* March 21, 1936, pp. 26–36; March 28, 1936, pp. 43–49.

Cragin, John H. *Christ Came as Promised.* Kenwood, N.Y.: By the author, 1895.

Dixon, William Hepworth. *New America.* Philadelphia: J. B. Lippincott & Co., 1867.

———. *Spiritual Wives.* Philadelphia: J. B. Lippincott & Co., 1868.

Eastman, Hubbard. *Noyesism Unveiled: A History of the Sect Self-Styled Perfectionists; with a Summary View of Their Leading Doctrines.* Brattleboro, Vt.: By the author, 1849.

Edmonds, Walter D. *The First Hundred Years: 1848–1948. 1848, Oneida Community; 1880, Oneida Community, Limited; 1935, Oneida Ltd.* [Oneida, N.Y.: Oneida Ltd., 1948].

Ellis, Havelock. *Sex in Relation to Society.* Vol. VI: *Studies in the Psychology of Sex.* Philadelphia: F. A. Davis Co., 1911.

Ellis, John B. *Free Love and its Votaries.* New York: United States Publishing Co., 1870.

Estlake, Allan. *The Oneida Community: A Record of an Attempt to Carry out the Principles of Christian Unselfishness and Scientific Race-Improvement.* London: George Redway, 1900.

BIBLIOGRAPHY

Hinds, William Alfred. *American Communities.* Oneida, N.Y.: Office of the *American Socialist,* 1878.

Lowenthal, Esther. "Labor Policy of the Oneida Community, Limited." *Journal of Labor Economy,* XXXV (1927), 114–26.

McGee, Anita Newcomb. "An Experiment in Human Stirpiculture." *American Anthropologist,* o.s., IV (1891), 319–25.

Miller, George N. *After the Sex Struck, or Zugassent's Discovery.* Boston: Arena Publishing Co., 1895.

Noyes, Corinna Ackley. *The Days of My Youth.* Kenwood, N.Y.: By the author, 1960.

Noyes, George Wallingford, ed. *John Humphrey Noyes: The Putney Community.* Oneida, N.Y.: By the author, 1931.

———, ed. *Religious Experience of John Humphrey Noyes, Founder of the Oneida Community.* New York: Macmillan Co., 1923.

Noyes, Hilda Herrick, and Noyes, George Wallingford. "The Oneida Community Experiment in Stirpiculture." Scientific Papers of the Second International Congress of Eugenics, 1921. *Eugenics, Genetics and the Family.* Vol. I, pp. 374–86. Baltimore: Williams & Wilkins Co., 1923.

Noyes, John H[umphrey]. *The Berean: A Manual for the Help of Those who Seek the Faith of the Primitive Church.* Putney, Vt.: Office of the *Spiritual Magazine,* 1847.

Noyes, John Humphrey. *Confessions of John H. Noyes, Part I: Confession of Religious Experience: Including a History of Modern Perfectionism.* Oneida Reserve, N.Y.: Leonard & Co., Printers, 1849. Part II was never published.

———. *History of American Socialisms.* Philadelphia: J. B. Lippincott & Co., 1870.

———. *"The Way of Holiness." A Series of Papers Formerly Published in the Perfectionist, at New Haven.* Putney, Vt.: J. H. Noyes & Co., 1838.

Noyes, Pierrepont [B.] *My Father's House: An Oneida Boyhood.* New York: Farrar & Rinehart, Inc., 1937.

Noyes, Pierrepont B. *A Goodly Heritage.* New York: Rinehart & Co., Inc., 1958.

———. *The Pallid Giant: A Tale of Yesterday and Tomorrow.* New York: Fleming H. Revell Co., 1927.

———. *While Europe Waits for Peace: Describing the Progress of Economic and Political Demoralization in Europe during the Year of American Hesitation.* New York: Macmillan Co., 1921.

Parker, Robert Allerton. *A Yankee Saint: John Humphrey Noyes and the Oneida Community.* New York: G. P. Putnam's Sons, 1935.

Robie, W. F. *The Art of Love*. Ithaca, N.Y.: Rational Life Publishing Co., Inc., 1925.

Robinson, C. E. [C. R. Edson]. "Communism: Oneida Community." *Manufacturer and Builder,* XXV (1893), 282–83; XXVI (1894), 94–95.

Van de Warker, Ely. "A Gynecological Study of the Oneida Community." *American Journal of Obstetrics and Diseases of Women and Children,* XVII (1884), 785–810.

Wayland-Smith, Francis [Gerald Thorne]. *Heaven on Earth: A Realistic Tale*. New York: Lovell Brothers & Co., 1896.

———. *Materialism and Christianity*. Kenwood, N.Y.: By the author, 1906.

———. *Shall We Choose Socialism?* Kenwood, N.Y.: By the author, 1907.

Wells, H. G. *The Future in America: A Search After Realities*. New York: Harper and Bros., 1906.

Pamphlets

Cragin, George, ed. *Faith-Facts; or a Confession of the Kingdom of God and the Age of Miracles*. Oneida Reserve, N.Y.: Leonard & Co., Printers, 1850.

Handbook of the Oneida Community: Containing a Brief Sketch of its Present Condition, Internal Economy and Leading Principles. No. 2. Oneida, N.Y.: Oneida Community, 1871.

Handbook of the Oneida Community, 1875. Oneida, N.Y.: Office of the *Oneida Circular,* [1875].

Handbook of the Oneida Community, with a Sketch of its Founder and an Outline of its Constitution and Doctrines. Wallingford, Conn.: Office of the *Circular,* 1867.

Noyes, George W[allingford]. *The Oneida Community; Its Relation to Orthodoxy: Being an Outline of the Religious and Theological Applications of the Most Advanced Experiment (in Applied Ethics) Ever Made in Any Age or Country*. N.p.: Fielding Star Print, [191?].

Noyes, John Humphrey. *Dixon and His Copyists: A Criticism of the Accounts of the Oneida Community in "New America," "Spiritual Wives" and Kindred Publications*. Wallingford, Conn.: The Oneida Community, [1871].

———. *Essay on Scientific Propagation*. Oneida, N.Y.: Oneida Community, [187?].

———. *Male Continence*. Oneida, N.Y.: Office of the *Oneida Circular,* 1872.

———. *Salvation from Sin: The End of Christian Faith*. Wallingford, Conn.: Oneida Community, 1866.

———. *The Doctrine of Salvation from Sin, Explained and Defended.* Putney, Vt.: By the author, 1843.

[Noyes, John Humphrey]. *Slavery and Marriage. A Dialogue.* N.p.: [By the author?], 1850.

Noyes, T[heodore] R. *Report on the Health of Children in the Oneida Community.* Oneida, N.Y.: [Oneida Community?], 1878.

[Oneida] Association. *Second Annual Report of the Oneida Association: Exhibiting Its Progress to February 20, 1850.* Oneida Reserve, N.Y.: Leonard & Co., Printers, 1850.

[Oneida Association]. *Bible Communism: A Compilation from the Annual Reports and Other Publications of the Oneida Association and Its Branches; Presenting, in Connection with Their History, a Summary View of Their Religious and Social Theories.* Brooklyn, N.Y.: Office of the *Circular,* 1853.

———. *First Annual Report of the Oneida Association: Exhibiting its History, Principles, and Transactions to January 1, 1849.* Oneida Reserve, N.Y.: Leonard & Co., Printers, [1849].

———. *Mutual Criticism.* Oneida, N.Y.: Office of the *American Socialist,* 1876.

———. *Third Annual Report of the Oneida Association: Exhibiting Its Progress to February 20, 1851.* Oneida Reserve, N.Y.: Leonard & Co., Printers, 1851.

[Oneida Community]. *The Oneida Community: A Familiar Exposition of Its Ideas and Practical Life.* Wallingford, Conn.: Office of the *Circular,* 1865.

Oneida Community, Limited. *By-Laws of the Oneida Community, Ltd., Together with an Act to Provide for the Organization and Regulation of Certain Business Corporations Passed by the Legislature of New York, June 21, 1875.* [Oneida] Community, N.Y., 1881.

———. *Oneida Community, 1848–1901.* N.p., n.d.

———. *The Oneida Community: Its Business Ideals.* N.p., [1910?].

Wayland-Smith, Louis. *Reminiscences.* Kenwood, N.Y.: By the author, 1955.

Periodicals

American Socialist. Oneida, N.Y. Vols. I–IV, 1876–79.

Circular. Brooklyn, N.Y., Oneida, N.Y., and Wallingford, Conn. Vols. I–XII, 1851–64; Vols. I–VII (n.s.), 1864–70.

Community Quadrangle. Kenwood, N.Y. Vols. I–V, 1926–30.

Community Quadrangle (2d ser.). Kenwood, N.Y. January–September/October, 1938 (mimeographed).

Daily Journal of Oneida Community. Oneida, N.Y. Vols. I–III, 1866–67.

BIBLIOGRAPHY

Free Church Circular. Oneida Reserve, N.Y. Vols. III–IV, 1850–51.

Kenwood Kronicle. Kenwood, N. Y. 1894–96 (mimeographed).

Kenwood Kronicle (2d ser.). [Kenwood, N.Y.?]. April 18, 1898–May 18, 1899.

O.C. Daily. Oneida, N.Y. Vols. IV–V, 1867–68.

Oneida Circular. Oneida, N.Y. Vols. VIII–XIII, 1871–75.

Perfectionist. New Haven, Conn. Vols. I–II, 1834–36.

Perfectionist. Putney, Vt. Vol. III, 1843–44.

Perfectionist and Theocratic Watchman. Putney, Vt. Vols. IV–V, 1844–46.

Quadrangle. Kenwood, N.Y. Vols. I–VII, 1908–14.

Spiritual Magazine. Putney, Vt., and Oneida Reserve, N.Y. Vols. I–II, 1846–50.

Witness. Ithaca, N.Y., and Putney, Vt. Vols. I–II, 1837–43.

Unpublished Works

Barron, H[elen] M. Memorandum dictated to H[ope] E. A[llen], May 24, [19]32. Historical collection, Mansion House library, Kenwood, N.Y.

Gadsby, Edward N., Jr. "Oneida Limited: The Implementation of a Social Creed." Bachelor's thesis, Amherst College, 1957.

Kinsley, Jessie. Diary, 1914–18. Private collection of Jane Kinsley Rich, Kenwood, N.Y.

Noyes, H[arriet] A. "History of the Printing Business of the O[neida] C[ommunity]." MS, [1875?]. Historical collection, Mansion House library, Kenwood, N.Y.

Noyes, Hilda Herrick, comp. Collection of MSS on the Oneida Community and the Oneida Community, Limited. Private collection of Mrs. Adèle Noyes Davies, Toronto, Can.

Noyes, Holton V. "History of the Oneida Community, Limited: 1880–1925." Taken from the minutes of the board of directors, with annotations by the author. MS, 1930. Private collection of the late Stephen R. Leonard, Sr., and Stephen R. Leonard, Jr., Kenwood, N.Y.

Noyes, John Humphrey. "Niagara Journal." Stone Cottage, Clifton, Ontario. MS, 1881. Private collection of the late Stephen R. Leonard, Sr., and Stephen R. Leonard, Jr., Kenwood, N.Y.

Oneida Family Register. MS listing names and personal data for the first 111 persons who joined the Oneida Community. Historical collection, Mansion House library, Kenwood, N.Y.

Raynsford, James Willard, Jr. "Pierrepont B. Noyes: American Rhineland Commissioner." Bachelor's thesis, Williams College, [1942?].

BIBLIOGRAPHY

"Record." A manuscript record of daily events at the Oneida Community, from January 1, 1863, to September 15, 1864. Historical collection, Mansion House library, Kenwood, N.Y.

Religious diary, 1851–54. Author's name withheld. Private collection of the late Stephen R. Leonard, Sr., and Stephen R. Leonard, Jr., Kenwood, N.Y.

Index

INDEX

INDEX

INDEX